CAMBRIDGE LIBRARY COLLECTION

Books of enduring scholarly value

Maritime Exploration

This series includes accounts, by eye-witnesses and contemporaries, of voyages by Europeans to the Americas, Asia, Australasia and the Pacific during the colonial period. Driven by the military and commercial interests of powers including Britain, France and the Netherlands, particularly the East India Companies, these expeditions brought back a wealth of information on climate, natural resources, topography, and distant civilisations. Their detailed observations provide fascinating historical data for climatologists, ecologists and anthropologists, and the accounts of the mariners, experiences on their long and dangerous voyages are full of human interest.

Narrative of a Voyage to the Ethiopic and South Atlantic Ocean, Indian Ocean, Chinese Sea, North and South Pacific Oceans in the Years 1829–31

Abby Jane Morrell (b. 1809) was the wife of ship captain and explorer Benjamin Morrell (1795–1839). During the nineteenth century it became more common for women to join their husbands on voyages, and Abby insisted on accompanying her husband on his fourth voyage. They left America for the Pacific in 1829 on board the *Antarctic*, which visited the Auckland Islands and Pacific Islands in search of commercial gain, before returning via the Azores in 1831. First published in 1833, this is Abby's account of their journey. It was ghostwritten by the American author Samuel Knapp (1783−1838) and followed the publication of Benjamin Morrell's own account as part of *A Narrative of Four Voyages* (also reissued in this series). It includes an account of the violent conflicts with the inhabitants of some of the Pacific Islands, and also contains Abby's comments on the 'amelioration of the condition of American Seamen'.

T0381609

Cambridge University Press has long been a pioneer in the reissuing of out-of-print titles from its own backlist, producing digital reprints of books that are still sought after by scholars and students but could not be reprinted economically using traditional technology. The Cambridge Library Collection extends this activity to a wider range of books which are still of importance to researchers and professionals, either for the source material they contain, or as landmarks in the history of their academic discipline.

Drawing from the world-renowned collections in the Cambridge University Library and other partner libraries, and guided by the advice of experts in each subject area, Cambridge University Press is using state-of-the-art scanning machines in its own Printing House to capture the content of each book selected for inclusion. The files are processed to give a consistently clear, crisp image, and the books finished to the high quality standard for which the Press is recognised around the world. The latest print-on-demand technology ensures that the books will remain available indefinitely, and that orders for single or multiple copies can quickly be supplied.

The Cambridge Library Collection brings back to life books of enduring scholarly value (including out-of-copyright works originally issued by other publishers) across a wide range of disciplines in the humanities and social sciences and in science and technology.

Narrative of a Voyage to the Ethiopic and South Atlantic Ocean, Indian Ocean, Chinese Sea, North and South Pacific Oceans in the Years 1829–31

ABBY JANE MORRELL

CAMBRIDGE
UNIVERSITY PRESS

CAMBRIDGE UNIVERSITY PRESS

Cambridge, New York, Melbourne, Madrid, Cape Town,
Singapore, São Paolo, Delhi, Mexico City

Published in the United States of America by Cambridge University Press, New York

www.cambridge.org
Information on this title: www.cambridge.org/9781108049771

© in this compilation Cambridge University Press 2012

This edition first published 1833
This digitally printed version 2012

ISBN 978-1-108-04977-1 Paperback

Sloan. Pinx.^t

Gimber & Dick, Sculp.^t

ABBY JANE MORRELL.

Miller Print

New York. J & J. Harper.

NARRATIVE OF A VOYAGE

TO THE

ETHIOPIC AND SOUTH ATLANTIC OCEAN, INDIAN OCEAN, CHINESE SEA, NORTH AND SOUTH PACIFIC OCEAN,

IN THE YEARS 1829, 1830, 1831.

BY ABBY JANE MORRELL,

WHO ACCOMPANIED HER HUSBAND, CAPT. BENJAMIN MORRELL, JR.,
OF THE SCHOONER ANTARCTIC.

"If all our care
Gives us a gentle husband, one that binds,
No galling yoke, happy our life indeed."

"I to Iolcos ploughed the watery way,
By fondness rather than by prudence led."

NEW-YORK:

PUBLISHED BY J. & J. HARPER,
NO. 82 CLIFF-STREET,

AND SOLD BY THE BOOKSELLERS GENERALLY THROUGHOUT THE
UNITED STATES.

1833.

TO MY COUNTRYWOMEN,

THE HAPPIEST OF THEIR SEX,

BORN IN A LAND OF LIBERTY,

EDUCATED IN A KNOWLEDGE OF VIRTUE AND TRUE
INDEPENDENCE,

SINGLE BY CHOICE, OR WEDDED WITH THEIR OWN CONSENT,

FRIENDS TO THE BRAVE, AND PATRONS TO
THE ENTERPRISING,

THIS HUMBLE NARRATIVE OF A LONG VOYAGE,

WITH SOME INCIDENTAL REMARKS,

IS

RESPECTFULLY AND AFFECTIONATELY DEDICATED,

BY THEIR OBEDIENT SERVANT,

A. J. M.

PREFACE.

When I took up my pen to prepare my journal for publication, I intended to make nothing more than a plain narrative of the events of my voyage, interspersed with such general remarks as might suggest themselves to my mind. But as I proceeded, I felt an irrepressible desire to make some observations on a subject which has become an object of no small interest to philanthropic sympathy—I mean the amelioration of the condition of American seamen. I believe that their habits can be reformed; and it requires no arguments to prove how much this reformation would subserve the best interests of commerce.

It may be thought strange that a woman should take up a subject so foreign to those which generally occupy the attention of her sex. It was, however, deeply impressed on my mind that, being a woman, I was in some measure better qualified to offer a few suggestions on this subject than any one engaged in the navy or the merchant service. A writer so situated might be suspected of wishing to effect promotion or of seeking employment; and knowing the dislike the public have to remarks coming from a quarter where interest or prejudice may be mingled with the information offered, I thought they might at least expect sincerity from me. With all my earnestness to make these remarks, I tremble when I think I am about to offer them for the consideration of the public. Perhaps they will listen to me kindly. It has been said, that when Napoleon was brooding over

his disasters no one dared approach him but a pet child,
who played around him and induced him to take nour-
ishment and repose.   Let the public therefore consider
me in the capacity of the child ; and if there be any force
in my suggestions, they will go for what they are worth ;
if there be none, why they will pass off with a smile.

It is seldom, indeed, that a female can know any
thing upon this subject ; but as I have had some opportunity of becoming acquainted with it, I hope I may be
excused for venturing to give my opinion.   I should
be proud to be one of the humble instruments in im-
proving the condition and raising the moral and intellectual standard of that race of men which ever has
and ever will share in the prosperity and glory of our
country.   In life I would ask no higher gratification
than to learn that the work of reform was going on suc-
cessfully ; and desire no other earthly honour after
death than an inscription on my tombstone declaring
that the ashes of the mariner's friend repose beneath.

                                        A. J. M.

New-York, January, 1833.

CONTENTS.

CHAPTER IV.

CHAPTER V.

CHAPTER VI.

CHAPTER VII.

NARRATIVE.

CHAPTER I.

The Author's Birth—Education—Marriage—Voyage with her
Husband—Death and Burial at Sea—Bonavista—St. Jago—
Blue Beard's Castle—Crossing the Equator—Sickness on
Board the Antarctic—Tristan D'Acunha—Storm at Sea—
Island of Desolation—Character of a good Ship-master.

PERHAPS I owe the public an apology for
appearing before them as an author. To become
one was not my intention when, by the kindness of my husband, I was permitted to take a
voyage with him into far distant seas; but as I
have seen much and suffered much, I have been
advised to give my narrative to my friends through
the press, hoping it might afford some amusement
to them as well as profit to myself. Another
argument had much weight with me, which was,
that I should thus be relieved of the necessity of
answering questions frequently put to me by my
friends and acquaintance when not in health, to
run over all the adventures of my travels; and I
thought, too, with the Moor of Venice, that if parts
and parcels of my "hair-breadth 'scapes" would,
at times, so much affect those I loved as I often
found they did, the whole story told at once

would move them to some kind attention to, and affectionate remembrance of, myself.

It may be asked, who is the person that offers us her narrative ? In this the reader shall be gratified, for short and simple are the domestic annals of one who has not reached her twenty-fourth year. My maiden name was Abby Jane Wood. I am the daughter of Capt. John Wood, of New-York, who died at New-Orleans on the 14th of November, 1811. He was at that period master of the ship Indian Hunter, of New-York. He died when I was so young, that if I please myself with thinking that I remember him, I could not have been a judge of his virtues ; but it has been a source of happiness to me that he is spoken of by his contemporaries as a man of good sense and great integrity.

I was born on the 17th of February, 1809, in the city of New-York. My early education was plain and regular in those branches then taught in respectable schools in my native city. At my father's death, my mother placed the property which he left in the hands of a person who either by intention or mismanagement lost or retained the whole of it. This was a grievous affliction to my mother, as she was left with a family of helpless children to maintain. The belief that she was vilely robbed at first preyed upon her mind ; but the consolations of religion lifted her above all her troubles, and she found the promises of the Gospel true, that, " I will be a husband to the widow and a father to the orphan." In 1814 my mother married Mr. Burritt Keeler, a gentle-man of a kind and generous disposition, which has been manifested, not only to my mother, but to her children which she brought him at the time

of their union. I can say,—and I think it my
duty not to pass over the fact in this narrative,—
that I feel towards my step-father as we should
to those to whom we owe our existence, and to
whom we are indebted for that paternal care
which springs from the laws of nature and the
social relations of life.

The days of my childhood passed away as those
of other children, and brought with them the
pleasures and pains, common to that season of
life : one of my greatest enjoyments, and one
which has fastened most strongly on my mind, was
derived from a constant attendance on Sundays
at St. Paul's or Trinity Church. I often called
to mind these images, while floating upon the
vast ocean, and considered the value of early
instruction in religion; the house of prayer and
the heaven-breathing music, with the solemn voice
of holy men, and the precepts that fell from their
lips, seemed all to come up, as it were, before me,
and extend the worship of God all around, while
the mighty abyss of waters was beneath us. The
impressions made in youth upon the eye or the
ear, as well as those upon the heart, live long
upon the mind ; and there is nothing like distance
from home, or solitude and danger, to brighten up
these images. The mind seems to find new
fountains of refreshing waters from these recollections, which, while they purify and elevate,
strengthen the soul for the hour of trial.

Early in the year 1824 my cousin, Capt. Benjamin Morrell, returned from a long voyage to the
Pacific Ocean. I had not seen him since I was
five years of age, and had hardly the slightest
recollection of him. At our first interview I felt
a friendship for him that I had never felt for any

one before. His personal appearance, his gentlemanly manners, and humane disposition, which
was seen in his benignant face, as well as his adventures, had an effect upon my mind that I did
not think of lightly. His visits to our house were
constant for several weeks, when he offered me
his hand, and, the match being acceptable to my
parents, we were married on the 29th of June.
A short time after this event he informed me that
he was soon to sail on a two years' voyage. I
knew when I married him that I was to be the
wife of a sea-faring man, but it was impossible
for me to realize the distress of separation. Only
a little month had passed away when my husband
proposed to sail, and on the 18th of July this
dreadful separation took place. I was calm, for
it was a matter of duty and necessity ; but no
one who has not felt them can tell the pangs of
such a separation. A bride of fifteen to see her
husband depart for such a length of time requires
more or less than the fortitude of woman.

He left me, and for many nights my dreams
were of him, on a boundless ocean, tossed by
storms or ingulfed in the deep. To these gradually succeeded dreams of his being wrecked on
desolate islands, and subject to all the violence of
savage men. My feelings were probably the same
as every good wife experiences when her spouse
has left her for distant lands ; but I was so young
that I had never run over in my mind any thing
of this kind before, and all was as new as distressing. At another time he would, in my imagination, be lying on a bed of sickness, with no one to
give him a cup of cold water to cool his parched
lips, or to render him a single act of kindness.
"He has good sailors," said my friends. I was

silent, but thought to myself, "A sailor is not a wife." In this manner passed my nights and days, until my husband came home, which was on the 9th of May, two months short of the time fixed for his return. I had heard that the vessel in which he sailed had arrived, and on going to a friend's with my sister to ascertain the fact, I met my husband in the street. Our meeting was such as might be imagined by one who has been separated from a beloved husband so long. All my anxieties were at an end—all my hopes were realized—my happiness was complete. There is a concentration of feeling, I may say of affection, after such an absence, that none but the wife of a mariner can know. I had dwelt upon the loves of those separated by the Crusades ; but the longer they were gone, and the more perilous their adventures, so much the more delightful was the story. Yet it was not so to those mourning the long absence of him who roamed into far-distant lands, carrying with him plighted vows and everlasting affections. I have often thought that the ages of chivalry had not gone, as far as woman's love was a part of it. I believe human nature is the same in every age and nation, and all of good hearts feel alike, whether it is called romance or fact. I can say for myself, that I have felt more than I have ever known described.

After several European voyages,—during which we had a son, who, in his mother's eyes, bore a striking resemblance to his father,—in June, 1828, my husband sailed again for the South Seas. The separation seemed worse than before, and I then came to the determination that if he ever went to sea again I would accompany him. This voyage

was not so long as I thought it would have been ;
he was gone but little more than a year, for he returned on the 14th of July, 1829. He had been
but a short time on shore, however, when he
planned another voyage to the Pacific. I had
determined to go, and ventured to mention it to
him. At first he would not hear a word of it, but
when I insisted, as far as affectionate obedience
could insist, he detailed to me all the evils of a
sea-faring life. I remained fixed, and he at last
reluctantly yielded ; and when he had agreed to
it, he put the best side outwards. I was now
engaged in making preparations for a two years'
voyage, which was no small affair, for many
things were to be thought of in such preparations.
    All things being ready, on the 2d day of
September, 1829, we embarked on board the
schooner Antarctic, and set sail. The crew con-
sisted of twenty-three good sailôrs. A fine breeze
wafted us from the shores of my native country,
and I soon began to feel the importance of my
undertaking, as it regarded myself. I had left
my boy behind me, and distance seemed to make
me more anxious for his welfare. I knew he was
in good hands, but he was not in my own ; I
knew my dear mother would do every thing for
him that I could, but nothing will satisfy a mother
in regard to her offspring, but her own care.
While I was thinking of these things I began to
grow sea-sick. The sensation can never be described ; it prostrates sense, fortitude, feelings, and
reduces the adult to the baby. On the morning
of the second day I came on deck, and all was one
boundless expanse of ocean ; the impression was
one of magnificence, if my situation would not
allow it to be one of pleasure. All was new to

me ; the management of the ship, the discipline of the sailors, &c. ; all were so respectful towards my husband and myself, and so gentle towards each other, that one would have thought them a band of brothers.

I often amused myself in gazing at the huge whales that tumbled about and sported in the deep around our vessel, seeming not to regard her any more than they would an egg-shell floating by them. The dolphins, too, so much admired by the ancients, as books tell us, were seen in great numbers. They were often noticed pursuing the flying-fish, who, to avoid their pursuers, arose from the water and kept in the air for the space of half a minute or more, and then fell into the water again ; sometimes they would fly on our deck, and we picked up some that would weigh nearly half a pound.

My sickness continued, and I was quite exhausted by it ; but I had embarked at my own solicitation, and I did not suffer myself for a moment to repent, nor complain. I considered that it was my duty to bear up as cheerfully as I could. My husband saw with pain how much I endured, and did every thing in his power to make me comfortable ; but after all his care, I suffered much more than I complained of. I walked until I felt faint, got a little better, and then took up a book ; but in a few moments the lines would swim before my eyes, and a tale of the deepest interest would affect me no more than the dullest story ever told by dozing senility. I have read of the stoics' bearing pain without any emotion, and wearing a smile on their countenances while their flesh was torn with pincers : it might have been so, but I think the most famed of that sect

would have looked a little pale in a fit of sea-
sickness.

On the 29th of September, one of the crew,
Francis Patterson, died, after a very severe illness,
supposed to have been brought on by having
drunk too freely of ardent spirits in the early part
of his life, and now leaving off suddenly. My
husband had shipped his crew upon condition
that they should abstain from all ardent spirits,
unless as medicine to the sick.   He was the first
captain, I believe, that ever shipped a crew for so
long a voyage on such terms ; and he found his
account in it as a navigator, without saying any
thing of the good done to the morals of these
generally improvident men without such wholesome restraints.   Patterson had reached the age
of sixty-three, and had too long been in the use of
ardent spirits to live many years, whether he ab-
stained or not.   He was a fine old sailor, and had
only this single failing, which is indeed a great
one, on the sea or on shore.

At four o'clock in the afternoon the funeral services of the deceased took place.   I supposed that
the body would be thrown overboard without
much ceremony, but it was not so ; the funeral
was the most solemn I ever witnessed.   The
body was laid out with great decency, and then
enveloped in a hammock and sewed up.   About
fifty pounds of stones were secured to the feet,
concealed by the hammock in which it was
wrapped, for the purpose, as I presumed, of sinking the body deep in the ocean.   The corpse was
extended upon a plank on the rail at the gang-
way, and all hands were called around, on the
right side of the ship, to witness the solemn
scene, and to join in the prayers to be offered up.

The colours were set half-mast, and the topsails
and top-gallant-sails were settled down on the
cap. Prayers were then read. The hardy crew
were deeply affected at the scene. The furrows
in their sunburnt faces were wet with tears.
Never before had I beheld so solemn a group:
I thought they had the kindest hearts of any set
of men that ever lived. The prayers being over,
a gun was fired from the bows of the schooner,
and the body instantly launched into the bosom
of the ocean. The plunge was a dreadful shock
to my feelings! I had heard the first shovelful
of earth thrown upon a coffin in a grave-yard,
at home; that was heart-rending, but not so bad
as this plunging into the deep. To the grave-
yard a friend might repair, at some future day,
and linger over the ashes of the dead; might erect
a stone at his head, and compose the mind by
writing his virtues on the marble; but here in
this grave no mortal could tell where he was—the
unconscious waters had closed over him for ever!

I was awakened from my revery by the shrill
pipe of the boatswain, calling all hands to duty.
In an instant the sails were set, and we were
gliding onward. There was no longer any melancholy in the countenances of the brave seamen; every one seemed to look as if he had done
his duty, and had nothing to reproach himself
with. The mate took his log-book, and wrote
this sentimental epitaph: "Buried Francis Patterson this day, in latitude 16° 35′ north, and
longitude 26° 2′ west from Greenwich. He
died yesterday. The weather now fair, winds
light." "So sink the brave to rest," was my reflection; and it is no matter where they rest, if
they go down to the place thereof with the hopes
of a resurrection and a life to come,

The winds were light and variable until the 4th of October, when land was discovered on our starboard bow (I had now learned most of the sea-phrases). After land was announced by the sailor at the mast-head, my husband went up, and I watched his ascension without emotion, for I had become familiar to the climbing of the sailors; a month before I should have gone into fits to have seen him in what I then considered so dangerous a situation. The land proved to be St. Nicholas. The next day we saw the island of Bonavista, and in the afternoon we came to anchor in the harbour, about two miles from the town. It was pleasant for me again to see land, men, shipping, churches, &c.; things I had been accustomed to all my life till the last thirty-three days. There was a breeze came from the shore that seemed to me to be refreshing. These men and women, though not wondrously well-looking, appeared to me to be beauties. I had seen nobody but our shipmates for so many days— many days for a female sailor. These few days, on retrospection, appeared to me nearly as long as my life had been.

Early in the morning we received a visit from the health officer, and at ten o'clock my husband and myself went on shore. The officer took us up to the governor, who with his amiable family received us with great kindness, and made us acquainted with their friends. Kind attentions are at all times pleasant, but when one is away from home it is delightful indeed to meet with those who love to pay all the courtesies of life as if it was their pleasure and happiness to do so. My stay was short, but I shall long remember the politeness, yea, friendship of that accomplished

family. They attended me to the boat, their
servants bearing presents of such things as would
be wanted on our voyage. Our separation came :
we ladies embraced, and left each other with
tears. There is something in these transient
attachments which shows us that we were born
to do each other good, notwithstanding all the
evil there is in the world. We were soon out of
sight of these hospitable shores. I waved a last
adieu to friends whose kindness had made me love
them as sisters, and then I was long silent, while
our bark was moving on at the rate of eight or
nine miles an hour. There is something soothing in this rapidity of motion when our minds
have been agitated by a variety of thoughts and
feelings.

Early the next morning we made the islands
St. Jago and Mayo. We came to anchor in the
harbour of the former. The bottom, I noticed, was
a beautiful white sand. The American consul's
flag was flying about a mile and a half distant. We
soon went on shore, and were kindly received by
him. Mr. Merrill, the consul, took great pains to
give me all the information he could about the
place. My friends pointed out to me the ruins of a
castle, which they said was the residence of the
famous BLUE BEARD, in his time. This was no
doubt true, as this island and those in the neighbourhood were the rendezvous of the Bucaniers of
America, who, after having robbed the Spaniards
and others, came to these places for security. The
island abounds in vegetables common to tropical
regions, of which we took in a good stock, and
filled our casks with pure water.

We left these hospitable friends with regret,
and with light winds made the best of our way

towards the equator. We had, from day to day, frequent falls of rain, with quick and heavy thunder. Sometimes flash would follow flash until the heavens seemed in one continuous blaze. On the 23d of October we crossed the line, in longitude 22° 10 west. About 4 o'clock, P. M., I witnessed the amusing ceremony of a visit from Neptune. He came on board, not precisely with such a trident as he holds in classic paintings, nevertheless he did well enough for green hands, in which number I suppose he ranked me. With great good-nature he shaved a few of the crew who had never before crossed the equator ; and the sailors thought for the first time in his life he made all merry without being treated with one drop of ardent spirits. Although he did not pre-tend to have any power over a female sailor who had never crossed the equator, I thought it best to propitiate him with a few small presents, which seemed to be acceptable to the great monarch of the ocean. He understood English very well, although the Portuguese say that theirs is his mother-tongue. The English language, from the use made of it by the seafar -men of both the mother and the daughter, must have been far more familiar to him, for a century or two past, than any other tongue ; and from all appear-ances, he is likely to adopt it as his court lan-guage. These things are pleasant enough to pass away an hour ; and I have been at sea long enough to find that the art of managing sailors consists in keeping them temperate, industrious, cleanly, and cheerful. They are always obedient when healthy and comfortable.

We had now got into the south-east trade-winds, and the weather being pleasant, my husband began to exercise the crew in the management of the big guns, and in the use of small arms. The old tune of "Yankee Doodle," which was played when the men had closed their exercises, sounded very pleasant in my ears.

The voyage, with all its vicissitudes, had been pleasant until October 26th, when I was taken sick with an intermittent fever, and at the same time eleven of the crew and the officers in the cabin. Among our complement of men was a brother of mine, a discreet lad, with acquirements far above his years. He was of great assistance to my husband, as well as a great comfort to me. The disease advanced so rapidly that in five or six days nearly one-half of our crew were prostrate with it. My husband, who still had sound health, was so constantly employed in attending to his vessel and to the sick, that I verily believe he did not sleep two hours out of twenty-four during the sickness. The second day of November was a bad one to us all. I was very weak, and my senses had at times been wandering, yet I could perceive that fresh calamities had overtaken us ; but what they were was concealed from me. After my recovery, my husband told me that on that day he buried Samuel Gerry, and was fully impressed with the idea that his crew would nearly all of them die with the fever. The next day Daniel Spinney died ; but all was concealed from me. One after another was carried out of the cabin, but I dared not inquire, and no one ventured to explain. I saw my husband's heart was full of sorrow, but I asked no explanations, knowing that I could do no good. My husband, still thinking it might injure me to know the worst, was silent; and I, believing that questioning would

B

add to his grief, adopted the same course. I learned from my brother, after a while, however, who dropped hints now and then, what was going on. I lost all hope, and began to think that it was my fate to be buried in the Indian Ocean. The feverish dreams that flitted across my imagination were those of being pendent in mid-ocean, of being devoured by sharks, or of wasting whole ages in rising and sinking in a world of waters. No hopes of a future life could rid me of these feelings—they belong to poor human nature. The fever now left us all, and we had to struggle alone with weakness. For myself, I was drawn all up like a cripple; but by the kind attention of my husband I began to recruit, although I had still much to suffer; and despite the application of linaments and frictions, I was a long time in getting into an erect position. In so short a time will sickness bring down the firmest constitution.

Weak as we were, my husband determined on touching at Tristan d'Acunha, for the purpose of getting poultry and other fresh provisions, to raise the sick by such refreshments as experience would dictate were good for them to receive. We now saw the island for so many days the object of our wishes, and on the 15th of November sent a boat ashore on the north side, the only part inhabited. There were about seven or eight men and as many women, with families amounting to about twenty children, on the island. I was carried on dock as often as my health would permit, to take a look at the land and to catch a mild breeze. On the land, which is elevated to a tremendous height above the sea, we saw goats and hogs, and a great variety of beautiful birds, both of land and sea kind. The land seemed to me much like

that of St. Helena,—which we afterward saw,—
formed of high ridges and deep chasms, probably,
as my husband thought, of volcanic origin. The
whole shore seemed to be teeming with animated
nature. Shellfish, seal, sea-elephants, and wild-
fowl were found in great abundance. Excellent
fish, particularly a large kind of perch, were
furnished for our table. The right whale, particularly the female of that species, were playing
around the shores. At certain seasons they come
into as smooth waters as they can find, for they
dare not trust their young ones to a wide and
boisterous ocean until they have gained the
strength of some months from their birth. Affection seems not confined to our breathing atmosphere, but lives in the deep ocean—on its surface
—everywhere. God is love, and that love pene-
trates all his universe. That such a monster as
a whale should have a heart, and feel for its
progeny, seems strange, but would it not be stranger if such a body should be made without
affections?

There is a bay on the N.N.W. side of this
island, which is open to the north wind. The
beach is of black sand, and extremely beautiful,
upon which a boat may be hauled up at almost
any season of the year. There are two or three
sparkling cataracts upon the steeps, from which
excellent water is taken without difficulty.
Sometimes this is done by hose, without the necessity of landing the boat. The highlands are
covered with forests, bearing the appearance of
yew-trees. A great variety of plants grow on
this island, proving that it has a soil fit for almost
any kind of cultivation. It is free from reptiles
and wild beasts, and seems to have come up from

the ocean for the benefit of man, as he wanders across the mighty deep. Tristan d'Acunha, from my husband's observations, lies in latitude 37° 5′ 40″ S., and longitude 12° 7′ 15″ W. This and the two neighbouring islands have long been discovered. The other two are called Inaccessible Island, and Nightingale Island.

After getting a good store of hogs, sheep, fowls, and various kinds of vegetables on board, we sailed on our voyage. For a few days we had pleasant weather, when a gale struck us, which was the first of any magnitude that we had experienced since we left New-York. This was tremendous. Every moment I expected to be ingulfed in the ocean. Several times I was most violently thrown out of my berth by the surges of the sea. After blowing hard for two days, the gale abated on the 1st of December. We continued our course to the island of Desolation, with strong winds, and now and then a storm of hail and snow.

On the 5th of December, we were again cheered by the sound of " Land ahead !" and soon came into smooth water. We entered the harbour which was discovered by Capt. James Cook, the celebrated navigator, in 1776. No place in either hemisphere hitherto discovered, affords a better field for a naturalist than this. The seabirds are numerous, including several kinds of albatrosses—a greater variety than I ever saw before ; they were so thick around the vessel that they were in each other's way. Seals and seaelephants were once numerous here also.

From this romantic place we sailed for Lord Auckland's group. I now began to feel some appetite, and relished the delicacies we had on

board; but the fever had left me in a sad state.
I saw but little of my husband, as the weather
was boisterous, and he was confined most of his
time to the deck, as his officers were yet weak
and unable to do their duty. I was in constant
alarm for fear my husband would get sick, and it
was a mercy that he held out so well. A kind
Providence overrules our destinies; and I was
penetrated with gratitude to Heaven that he was
spared to be the protector of us all. If his gentleness and benevolence had won my heart, his
fortitude and bravery in the most trying scenes
excited my admiration; and, if I might be allowed
to say it, my pride was raised that he was capable of taking care of others as well as myself;
for I could see that the sailors were never dis-
couraged; they had such confidence in their
commander that they never thought of danger
when with him. The more feeble we are, the
more we confide in those who can protect us.

It is impossible for a woman to understand the
true character of her husband by only seeing him
in the domestic circle: she must watch him in
trying circumstances, and where she cannot be
called to counsel and advise, to form a just estimate of his qualifications for the discharge of
his public duties. In these trying situations my
husband was as calm as if only in the ordinary
discharge of his duties. He was by the dying
bed of the sick among the sailors, as well as by
mine, and seemed all energy, resignation, hope,
and decision. I could not but apply to him, however partial it may seem, the fine description of
the sailors' poet, of the commander of a ship
he sailed in to the Hellespont and Greece. The
genius of Falconer, his sufferings, and his un-

timely fate, as well as the inspirations of his
muse, endear him to every seaman's heart; his
Shipwreck is truly a sailor's epic.

"The lovely ship, with all her daring band,
To skilful Albert owned their chief command :
Though trained in boisterous elements, his mind
Was yet by soft humanity refined ;
Each joy of wedded love at home he knew,
Abroad, confess'd the father of his crew !
Brave, liberal, just ! the calm domestic scene
Had o'er his temper breathed a gay serene :
Him science taught by mystic lore to trace
The planets wheeling in eternal race ;
To mark the ship in floating balance held,
By earth attracted, and by seas repelled ;
Or point her devious track through climes unknown,
That leads to every shore and every zone.
He saw the moon through heaven's blue concave glide,
And into motion charmed th' expanding tide,
While earth impetuous round her axle rolls,
Exalts the watery zone, and sinks the poles ;
Light and attraction, from their genial source,
He saw still wandering with diminished force ;
While on the margin of declining day
Night's shadowy cone reluctant melts away,
Inured to peril, with unconquered soul,
The chief beheld tempestuous oceans roll :
O'er the wild surge, when dismal shades preside,
His equal skill the lonely bark could guide ;
His genuis, ever for th' event prepared,
Rose with the storm, and all its dangers shared."

CHAPTER II.

FREQUENTLY on our passage from the island of Desolation to Lord Auckland's group, we could not keep a fire to cook any thing, for the waves often swept over us; and our sails were splitting and spars were falling around us every day. It was on the 29th of December that we reached this group, and at eleven in the morning the crew went on shore to get shellfish and other things that we wanted, while the vessel was riding safely at anchor in a fine harbour. I amused myself in listening to the sweet notes of the ten thousand beautiful birds warbling among the forest trees, within fifty yards from the stern of the Antarctic. I had been assisted to the deck by my husband and brother, and weak as I was, I felt new life at the scene. In the ecstasy of the

moment, I felt that all the flowers were opening
to receive me—that the birds sang a joyous welcome for me—and the " incense-breathing morn"
was charming to my senses. To one who has
escaped the dangers of the sea—who has been
long prostrate upon a sick-bed—a gleam of sun-
shine is reviving; but now all my senses were
banqueting at once. If ever gratitude to my
Maker penetrated my heart, it was at this moment; if ever I poured out that heart, it was at
such enjoyments as I now felt. Such moments
as these are an equivalent for long days and
nights of pain. The sea around me was full of
alabatrosses and aquatic birds of all sorts which
are found in a temperate climate. The land was
picturesque—the hills beginning to rise almost
from the water's edge, with deep valleys between
them, each terminating at the shore in small
caves. The forests were very luxuriant, and
showed the strength and fertility of the soil,
which was covered with numerous plants not
common to my own country. I noticed several
that I was acquainted with, and many that I did
not know. One plant here deserves to be particularly mentioned: it is a species of flax that
bears a yellow flower, and grows near the seashore, and sometimes far up the hills. The
threads of the heart are silky; and, in the opinion of my husband, it might be raised in our
southern states, and by its abundant growth and
easy cultivation soon supersede hemp-fields, as
well as those of flax. The season here at this
time answers to our July; though not uncom-
fortably warm at any part of the day, the ther-
mometer not rising above 65° at noon. The
land-birds were large brown and green paroquets,

large wood-pigeons, and a great variety of small birds. Among the latter there is a green bird, about the size of a robin, whose melody is so fine, and his notes so varied, that one might imagine himself regaled by a hundred different sorts of songsters at once. The animals here are mostly strangers to man, and have but little fear of him. It is seldom that they hear the murderous gun of the sportsman; and the ornithologist in his rambles around the globe has, perhaps, never been here to write the biographies of these tenants of the forest. The fish here are good, and can be had at all times.

On the 4th of January we sailed from the Auckland group; our vessel was in fine order, and we seemed to set out as on a new voyage. The group at which we were so much refreshed lies in south latitude 50° 40', and 166° 4' east longitude.

On the 6th of this month we saw the south cape of New-Zealand. The boats were sent to examine the shore, but found no fur-seal upon them, the obtaining of which was one object of the voyage. The boats continued to examine the shores of the south-east and east sides of Night Island. The winds were light and the weather fair, and on the 12th of January, at noon, we had a visit from the natives, who came off to us in a war-canoe, which contained about fifty men, two of whom were principal chiefs, from Flat Point. These chiefs were whimsically tattooed; their ears marked, and their bodies stained with red or blue. From all that we could learn, their chief occupation is war. They carry about them a greater variety of offensive and defensive weapons than most other savages. Their looks are

bold and fierce, and they have no small share
of martial dignity.   Like other savages they
delight in the war-song, and carry their phrensy
and fury to the greatest excess.   They have
been, as near as I could learn, cannibals, and
now, when prisoners are taken, they frequently
cut from them while alive pieces of flesh and
masticate it, to show their fury and fiendish joy
at their success.   Their dexterity in the use of
their war-clubs, spears, &c., is said to be surprising.   Their affections are strong ; they mourn
their dead with all those marks of phrensy so often
described to us as belonging to savage life.   They
cut themselves—tear their flesh—and utter the
most piercing cries.   Polygamy is allowed among
them ; a chief having two or three wives, or
perhaps as many as he wishes to maintain ; or
it may be, that the number marks the rank of the
warrior or chief.   The females are generally
quite young, many of them mothers at the age
of twelve or fourteen.   Ignorance is the mother
of superstition, and these savages have it to a
great extent.   Their priests are arbitrary, and
keep them in fear, being under that bondage
themselves.   I have marked that they observe
their fasts and their prayers from impressions
of fear.   The love of God is not known where
ignorance abounds ; it is that love, properly
known, that casteth out all fear.   Some of these
superstitions make them vigilant and daring, as
well as cautious ; they believe that the spirit of
him who was killed and devoured by his enemies
suffers everlasting punishment in the world of
spirits, but if rescued and buried his spirit ascends
to the abode of their gods.   This opinion generally prevails throughout all the southern hemi-

sphere among the savages. These savages have more curiosity than our North American Indian are said to have, for they examined the Antarcti with great scrutiny and apparent delight, and took their departure in the most peaceful manner. We continued the examination of the shores, holding frequent intercourse with the natives.

On the 19th of January we saw Cape Briton, and soon after came to anchor in the Bay of Islands, about five miles east of the missionary establishment, where we found several English whaling-ships, viz. the ship George, Captain Gray, from London ; the Royal Sovereign, Captain King, and the Thetis, Captain Gray, from the same place. These were skilful, enterprising navigators, and very gentlemanly men. They all treated us with the greatest kindness, and I dined on board of each in turn, and received every attention that could be paid to a female in a distant country, whose very situation excites some sympathy and great courtesy. It is pleasant, if it is even at the farthest side of the globe, to be where national prejudices are forgotten, and all are of the same family. It is impossible for those who speak the same language not at times to love one another.

On the 20th of January, 1830, the English captains, my husband, and myself, went to pay our respects to the good people of the missionary establishment. My heart was overflowing at being once more in the embraces of Christian friends. Oh ! there is religion in the world, said I, mentally, when I saw the accomplished females who had left all the comforts of society and the charms of friendship in England, to come to these shores of heathenish ignorance and ferocity, for the sake of extending the Redeemer's kingdom, putting their trust in him, and overcoming the vanities of this world. Their labours were incessant ; for they did not allow themselves more than eight hours out of the twenty-four for repose and meals. All the rest were devoted to civilizing and Christianizing the natives. The male missionaries work many hours in the field, clothed in duck frocks and trousers, with the natives, learning them to cultivate their lands. They then spend several hours in the day in teaching the natives to read and write, and to understand the precepts of our holy religion. The wives and daughters of these pious labourers are engaged in teaching the females to sew and to read. The natives are devout and tractable. These missionaries seemed to have as many under their care as they could readily teach, and their influence was spreading far and near, and is now extremely powerful. A few years ago not a ship's crew could land without arms and a guard, and perchance, some of them were massacred in attempting to get a little wood or water ; but now they may travel anywhere to the extent of a hundred miles around the missionary dwellings, and eat and sleep in security, without guard or arms, or without fear. When a vessel arrives the natives are seen flocking to the shore, extending their arms to receive the white men from a distant country, bringing with them the fruits of their agriculture in great quantities, at the lowest prices. A quarter of a dollar here, I am positive, would purchase more than could be had in the New-York market for two dollars.

The common kitchen-garden vegetables are excellent, and in fine variety ; some apples may be had, and the small meats and poultry are supplied in abundance. Beef is not as yet much in use, but soon will be raised, as much as will be required. When I thought of these changes, produced by such feeble means, I wondered how any one could doubt the truth and efficacy of the Christian religion. Here, without the shedding of one drop of blood, Christianity had been planted; it had been as the tree of life in a forest of the upas, and the healing in its leaves had brought out and spread abroad light and salubrity where once darkness and pestilence reigned.

The whole party remained with these good people until about four o'clock in the afternoon, when we proposed leaving; but they were anxious to have us all stay with them while we were on the coast. The captains declined, as they did not think it proper to sleep away from their vessels, for the wind often blows hard here, and sudden squalls are common, but my husband consented that I might stop for one night. Often when joining with them in their devotions I asked myself, can there be any thing selfish in this? is it not pure and undefiled religion before God? it can hardly be called before man, for there were no civilized men to observe them. How happy they seemed! indeed, how happy they were, although so far removed from the dear country of their birth and the friends of their childhood. Even prayer itself is purified on such an occasion and in such a place; it was no great stretch of the imagination for me to think myself joining in the devotions of those who had lived in paradise in primitive innocence.

I now felt myself recruiting very fast, for I could walk a few rods without assistance, my limbs beginning to come to a natural state of

feeling ; but inflexible duty would not suffer my
husband to linger here on any account. He came
for me on the following day, and I was obliged to
take a painful farewell of these holy people. Mr.
Davis and his daughters, Mr. Williams and his
wife and daughters, and some of the natives, came
to take their leave of me. They prayed for my
temporal and eternal happiness, and for my
friends, and then sang a hymn that went to my
soul, and waked up all its sympathies. They all
accompanied me to the beach, and with tears,
embraces, and kisses, I and my female friends
parted,—they to attend to duties, and I to be
tossed again by the winds and waves, to encounter new hardships, and to enjoy new adventures.
On my reaching the deck of the Antarctic I was
received by my brother and our brave tars with
three hearty cheers, which were repeated by the
crews of the English ships alongside of us, and to
close the scene these cheers were echoed and re-
echoed by a thousand native voices, in the canoes
and on shore.

The next day we could not sail as we expected,
the wind blowing too fresh from the north. The
natives, seeing this, were desirous that we should
again come on shore, and an invitation for us to
visit them came from the king and queen, which
was accepted. This was the 23d day of January,
1830. The boats of the Antarctic were prepared,
and those of the ships joined, amounting in all to
twelve whale-boats, handsomely manned. The
natives had expected us, and came in myriads to
see us. On touching the shore we were met
by KIPPY-KIPPY, the king ; the queen then approached, and extended her hand most courteously
to welcome an American woman to her territory.

Her appearance was affable and kind. After our greeting was passed, she waved a fan she held in her left hand, and at this signal more than seven thousand of her train, of both sexes, broke out into a song of joyous welcome; after which they gave three cheers that made the welkin ring. They then formed two double parallel lines, the females composing the inner, and the males the outer sections. As we advanced the females fell on their knees, and the males on one knee. I was carried on a sort of stage or chair, by six of their principal warriors, who proceeded with great state and solemnity, decorated with feathers of different kinds. Some of their ornaments were of surpassing beauty. The women all bore a green branch in their hands, and the heads of the men were ornamented with branches and feathers. When we came within fifty yards of the king's palace, the pathway was strewed with beautiful wild flowers, quite to the door, where we found elegant mats spread for at least ten yards square. The king now spread before us a superb banquet of the choicest fruits of his clime, and the young women entertained us with many songs, of no ordinary melody; after which the warriors gave us a war-dance for our amusement. There were at least two hundred of them. The king then came forward and made us a speech, and to my surprise, he spoke very good English. The substance of the oration was in praise of the missionaries. He said that before these good men came they knew nothing, but that now they were good men; that they could now lie down and sleep without fear of being killed by their enemies; that now they could sleep in peace; and that before these good men came, they had eaten human flesh, and thought it acceptable to their gods. The night coming on, I could not obtain all the information I could wish. I acquainted the queen that I must now leave her and go on board ; at which she clasped me in her arms, and kissed me several times. She made me many presents of elegant mats and delicate shells, when I took my departure, and was attended to the boats with great ceremony. The bows being directed to our vessels, the tars, both English and American, dropped their oars at a signal, and the boats were propelled like dolphins through the water.

As soon as we left the beach, the natives gave three cheers, which were answered by our men with great glee. In a few minutes we reached the Antarctic, where we found a great many canoes alongside, loaded with potatoes and hogs in abundance, presents from the king and queen. It would be difficult after this to make me believe that missionaries could do no good among savages; such as we saw would do good anywhere. In a few short years all within their influence had been softened, and every one was anxious to be more enlightened. Some had all the gentleness that attends the polite and good in any country. The terrific monarch of fierce warriors was now as courteous as a man could be, brought up in the bosom of polished society, and at the very first opportunity made an open acknowledgment of his obligations to religion and letters. I did not consider that these honours were paid to me as an individual, but to all females of my own country and to those of the English nation.

The next morning, January 24th, we took leave of all our English friends and the natives, got under way, and put to sea with a fresh breeze and a light rain, bound to Manilla. We continued on our voyage with occasionally thick weather and brisk breezes, until we reached the latitude of 1° 23′ north, and longitude 170° 2′ east. We now, February 16th, found ourselves in the north-east trade-winds, with fair weather, and on the 19th, in the morning, we saw Strong's Island, which lies in latitude 5° 58′ north, and longitude 162° 55′ east.

This island is about ten leagues in circumference, and of moderate height, as it appeared to us from the sea. The uplands are all covered with thick forest trees, and the low grounds with fruit trees. The appearance of the natives is wild; they have long hair, and their complexion is of a light copper colour. Their canoes are light, and from ten to fifty feet in length. They paddle them through the water with great skill and dexterity. They have a great partiality for trinkets, red paint, and all sorts of cutlery. An old iron hoop will purchase a plentiful supply of fruit—a strong proof that they are not often visited by Europeans, as Indians soon grow sagacious in their traffic. It is thought by navigators that this island contains sandal-wood and other valuables.

We continued our voyage with a fine wind and pleasant weather, occasionally seeing indications of land, such as grass, trees, sperm-whales, and many kinds of sea-birds.

On the 23d land was again seen from the mast-head, which proved to be seven small islands surrounded by a coral reef. These islands my husband said he believed had never been seen before; they certainly were not on any chart we had on board, and we were well provided with maps and charts. They are thickly inhabited, and are rich and fertile. We were in an unfrequented track, expecting to meet with shoals and new islands, and he therefore took the utmost precaution in keeping a look-out. Men were stationed at mast-head and other places, to mark the slightest appearance of danger. On the night of the 23d, breakers were discovered ahead, but by the timely precautions of my husband all difficulties were avoided, although we were in imminent danger, as I afterward understood from all the officers on board. I saw that the men had been much frightened, but my husband never talked of danger, nor did he ever permit me to think of it. I was, however, sadly alarmed at the time from his manner of command, and the thoughts of my child, my mother, and all my friends, rushed to my mind at once, and I felt that I was to be called to leave them; but Heaven ordered it otherwise—we were all saved. These hairbreadth escapes are better felt than described.

In the morning we took a view of the coral reef on which we had nigh been stranded. Within its circle were a large number of small islands, and within these we could easily distinguish four large high islands, which appeared to be very fertile, and covered with timber and fruit-trees. Several canoes were seen within the reef, filled with men, who seemed to wish us to anchor; but the number we saw made my husband think it might be hazardous to do so. One of the canoes ventured near us; the men were large, long-haired, and of a light mulatto colour. They were warlike in their appearance, but showed no signs of hostility. To these islands my husband gave the name of *Bergh's Group*, in honour of Edwin

Bergh, Esq., of New-York. These islands, also,
were not found upon any chart I have ever seen.

We kept on our course towards Manilla, and
on the morning of the 25th of February discovered another unknown island, surrounded by a
coral reef, which was but thinly inhabited; and
as we were not prepared to trade with the Indians,
we passed on without further notice at this time.

We continued on our course with fine north-
east trade-winds and delightful weather, until the
5th of March, when we arrived at the Straits
of St. Barnardino, and in the evening we came to
anchor in the entrance of the straits. In the
morning we passed through the straits, and
were gratified by seeing a fine country. Boats
were numerous, but we did not wish to be delayed by any intercourse with the natives. The
weather continued fine, and on the 10th of March,
we arrived at the port of Manilla, lying in longitude 121° 0' 9" east, latitude north 14° 35'. The
next morning we were visited by the health officer,
and in the afternoon landed. This island is of
great interest to the commercial world. It was
early settled by the Spaniards, who built a walled
city for security. The city within the walls is of
an irregular form, narrow at each end and wide
in the middle. A fine river runs through it, and
makes it susceptible of being kept clean; but
cleanliness is a rare virtue anywhere. The city
is tastefully built, many of the houses being wholly
of stone, and all of them have the first story of this
material. The roofs are flat, according to the
Spanish fashion, and most of the houses have a
piazza, for the convenience of air and exercise.
The streets are broad and airy, and the promenades, the most fashionable part of the city, are

elegant. The inhabitants are from twelve to sixteen thousand in number; probably the latter is nearest to the truth. There is but little appearance of business in the city, as most of the merchants, and all the mechanics, live without the walls. The men and women within seem to have no special employment; their whole business is to live and to enjoy themselves. There is an air of grace in the movements of Spanish females that marks them from most others. Devotion and amusement in such a place are the duties of the day. The churches are numerous, and make an imposing appearance. It is said that in this city there are more convents than in any other in the world of its size. There is one to almost every church, and the general voice of natives and foreigners declares that they are under excellent regulations. Looking at the convents as you pass along, you would imagine that one-third of the city was made up of these religious houses. The Catholic religion has one singular property, with all its parade and ceremony, in it; and that is, of making those who profess it quite content with it. They seldom disturb themselves with any abstruse speculations. There is something quite imposing in their forms, and the enlightened seem as much attached to them as the ignorant. I was born a Protestant, and I trust in heaven that I shall die a Protestant; but hereafter I shall have more charity for all who profess to love religion, whatever may be their creeds. The inmates of these nunneries live quite a different life from those without the walls of the edifice. They may be as busy at their devotions as those of the world at their pleasures, but not more so. This is an old coun-

try—older than my own; and all the habits and
manners of the people are as fixed as those from
whence they sprung. They have now no particular longings for Spain, but speak of that country as we do of England, although their governors
are appointed by the king; but he has no politics
in such a distant land, and they all enjoy a freedom, perhaps, not known in the mother country.
The island has had its vicissitudes, but its course
has been quiet and colonial, and the Spanish sway
has never been interrupted except when it was
taken by the British in 1762. It was ransomed
at a million sterling, which has never been paid.
     The suburbs of Manilla are crowded with in-
habitants, principally Chinese. These people are
skilful, and more industrious than the Spaniards
or the mixed breeds; and it is said that they
are honest,—comparatively speaking, I suppose.
The soil of this island is fertile and pretty well
cultivated; the sugar-cane grows abundantly,
and from it is drawn a great staple in their commerce. All the usual vegetables are plentiful;
but a principal part of the food of the poorer
classes consists of fish, of which the waters are
full of various wholesome kinds. The canoes, at
all times of the day and night, are seen on the
water with several fishermen in them, each carrying a light in the stern, which makes a most picturesque appearance. I could fancy myself looking upon one of our extensive meadows when
the glow-worm was showing her beautiful light,
and myriads of fireflies were on the wing.
Physicians say, that when the firefly and the
glow-worm are seen, the evening air has no
noxious vapour in it. These people on the water
never think whether the air is wholesome or not;

they were born to this task—it is their support—
and they must meet it. The fish are so abundant that they are used for manure at certain seasons of the year, and are said to make the ground
very fertile. To me, who was born and had
lived till this time in a country of frost and snow
for nearly half the year, it was delightful to be
where perpetual verdure smiled—where fruits
and flowers hung together by a law of nature,
and seemed to shadow forth the destiny of man—
when the old depart, and the young rush forward.

The palace at Manilla is a noble building, and
was once the residence of a viceroy; but the
hope of the Spanish nation in founding a great
eastern empire was never realized, and never can
be. It would not be difficult for a spirited people
to conquer the Philippine Islands, so far as
European power is concerned; but unborn ages
will probably pass away before these possessions
will become an object to any great maritime
power; yet so jealous is Spain of her Eastern
possessions, that a large body of troops is kept
in pay here as a standing army to repel any attempt to take these territories from her. The
government here, although arbitrary, is seldom
oppressive to its own members; but there have
been times in the history of Luconia in which
the Europeans, from some assumed apprehen-
sion, have made general massacres among the
Chinese on the island: one in the early history
of the colony, and the other about the middle of
the last century.

The Indian women here have, of course, some
share of civilization among them, and are superior to the men. If I have read aright, females
are always the leaders in civilization and Chris-

tianity; in this region they certainly have more
of an air of civilization than the men, and are
quite as industrious: however poor they may be,
there is no appearance of slatternliness about
them—every thing in their dress is neat, if not
worth ten cents. The Spanish lady is always a
high-bred woman, with no little of the spirit of
chivalry about her. Some of them have splendid
complexions of a bright orange tinge, with fine
eyes, and beautiful hair, well turned limbs, and a
graceful walk. If they had as much application
as genius, they would have no superiors in the
world. I have noticed their walk with admiration; it has a little of the martial staidness, with
the elastic tread of the Lady of the Lake. If
you could not say, as the immortal novelist and
poet has said of his heroine, that

> "A foot more light, a step more true,
> Ne'er from the heath-flower dash'd the dew;
> E'en the slight hair-bell reared its head
> Elastic from her airy tread:"

you could say firmness and lightness were never
more happily blended than in those females of
genteel society who walk the fine promenades of
this city. With them walking is as much of a
science and an art as playing upon the Spanish
guitar. I wish it was more attended to in my
own country. I have heard an anecdote from
good authority, which has always struck me as
containing a good and wholesome piece of satire.
An American female, some years ago, attended
by her husband—a naval hero,—took a voyage
to South America. Being of an adventurous
spirit, she travelled into the interior of the country, mounted on a milk-white horse, of the beau-

tiful South American breed ; and being dressed
in pure and elegant simplicity, and possessing a
splendid form and face that would have been
attractive anywhere, the inhabitants took her for
the Madonna, and bowed the knee and fell upon
the ground as she journeyed along. They followed her until she alighted from her horse,
when they immediately questioned her divinity
—there was nothing of the goddess in her movements—she had an awkward walk. It is not
those who walk the most that walk the best :
the spinner of street-yarn has seldom a majestic
or a beautiful gait.

The ladies of Manilla have generally each a
cabinet of beautiful shells, and a large collection
of birds, of splendid plumage. In both of these
curiosities the country is more rich than most
others. These shells are often tastefully arranged by the ladies in their leisure hours ; and
they have a method of keeping the plumage of
their birds as beautiful as it was in the groves
and in the rays of the sun. Great care is taken
to preserve them with such spices as will prevent
insects from injuring them.

During a great portion of the year Manilla is
healthy, but there are seasons when it is visited
by severe sicknesses. The cholera, now so dreadful a plague, and which is travelling all over the
world, has been among this people and carried
off thousands of them. It is rapid in its course,
and comes to a sudden crisis ; but when I was
there, it was more mortal in the country than in
the city. They think they have in some measure got the control of the disease ; but of this I
will not attempt to say much, as it has baffled
the wisest of the healing art in every country

through which it has marched. This people think not much of death, for there is a sort of Asiatic notion of predestination with them which makes them less attentive to the means of curing or warding off disease than with my own countrymen. If they are not so anxious to prevent death as we are, they are more attentive to the remains of the dead. The Catholics observe all the rites of the church in the article of death, and all the rites of sepulture. The bodies of the Spaniards are buried in the church or convent-yards, or under the churches, with every due and solemn form. Sometimes in the country, and not unfrequently in the churchyards of the city, you will see a tombstone, and by its side or head a large tamarind-tree, as a holy shade. It supplies the place of a weeping-willow in the United States, or of a yew-tree in England. The Indians are, if possible, more attentive to sepultural rites than the Spaniards; for they hold with ancient superstitions that the ghost is restless until the due burial rites are performed.

There are always some drawbacks in every country; even here, where you are regaled by the flowers of the orange and the fruit in the same breath, at times you are dreadfully annoyed by little red ants, that, like the frogs of Egypt, come up to the kneading-troughs, and to the very beds of the sensitive dons. It requires Yankee ingenuity to keep them from devouring you. The mosquitoes, at certain seasons, are very troublesome; they are large, sharp-set, and poisonous. This insect, I believe, is bred everywhere; or, at least, where nature is bountiful, and the soil luxuriant. They are an enemy, I am sure, that it is impossible to fight or avoid,

c

and those among whom they appear must contrive to act on the defensive only; by smoke
and nettings one may contrive to be made toler-
ably comfortable.

I dwell, perhaps, too long in this city, but I
must be excused; for it was here that I suffered
much in my mind, although I found good friends
among strangers. I have a painful tale to relate,
but one of which it is impossible for me to give
more than a faint outline. The cause of our
troubles and mortification has, sometime since,
gone to account for his acts and intentions to
another than an earthly tribunal; but I know no
reason why the truth, as regards the dead, should
not be told, if done without bitterness or a spirit
of revenge. As I hope for happiness, I will not
set down any thing in malice.

Soon after our arrival in this island, my husband became acquainted with the American consul at Manilla. He was a man of respectable acquirements, and of courteous manners. In a few
days, Mr. Morrell determined to fit out the Antarctic on a voyage to the Feejee Islands, for the
purpose of getting a cargo of tortoise-shell, biche-
de-mar, and other articles which are commonly
found there. We were all busy and happy in
getting ready for the voyage; and in the mean
time the consul's attentions to me were courteous
and friendly, but as yet respectful. At this time,
as I discovered afterward, my husband began to
suspect his intentions, and formed a new estimate
of his character; but I could not fairly understand this, as he was silent on most subjects of
his voyage. I conjectured, however, that all was
not right from his manner. A few days before
we were to sail, my husband intimated to me that

the Spanish government were opposed to *my*
going with him on his voyage to the Feejees, but
he could give no reason for it; nor could I conjecture why a harmless female could do any
injury among the savages of distant islands.
There was something extremely suspicious in it;
but the truth did not, at the first moment, flash
upon my mind, as it did afterward. I could not
suspect my husband of deceiving me, because the
voyage was not more dangerous in his and my
view than what we had already gone through
with. The next time I saw the consul all was
as plain as day to me, though I dared not express
myself freely to my husband, for fear of the consequences from his quick sense of injury, and his
high spirit as a brave man. And then, again,
my youth and ignorance of the world made me
fear that I had put a wrong construction upon
the consul's demeanour. I told my husband,
that, painful as our separation might be, if his interest and that of his owners required it, I could
and would make the sacrifice, and remain at
Manilla, if he would provide me a place of respectability to reside at while he was absent, so
that I should not be under the necessity of seeing
the consul. At length a residence was procured,
quite to my mind, with an English family, by
the name of Cannell. The firm under which
Mr. Cannell transacted business was Cannell and
Gellis. I had formed some acquaintance with
a niece of the first-named gentleman; she was a
well-informed young lady, of about twenty years
of age, and I had frequently seen the family of Mr.
Cannell. I had made up my mind to stay with
this worthy family, which I understood from my
husband had been vilely aspersed by the consul,

and represented as people wanting in character and integrity, within and without doors. I was nearly distracted, for I saw every day that my detention was, as I thought, a mere trick of the consul's; and, as he became more hateful in my eyes, I determined to steal a march on him, and go on the voyage to the Feejees, at all hazards. On the day the Antarctic was ready for sea, my husband had so arranged the matter that my brother was to take me on board; this was so privately done, that I did not think my persecutor would have found it out; but in this I was deceived. When my husband came on board, he brought with him two American captains and an English captain; Capt. Daggett, of Boston, Capt. Snow, from the same place, and Capt. Harris, from London; and also, the second captain of the port, an officer of the customs. I now thought all was safe; and, while congratulating myself that in a few minutes I should be beyond the pursuers power, I found, to my great distress, that the consul was on board. An altercation took place between him and my husband, in which he used every threat he could think of; and appealed to my husband as a man of honour, hypocritically assumed the tone of an injured man, and represented that he had pledged himself to the Spanish government that I should not go in the vessel, and that it would be ruin to him if he did not redeem his pledge; and added, that if this was not complied with, he must take the register of the Antarctic by force. This was, indeed, an idle threat; for we were out of the reach of the fort and gun-boats, and had a crew on board that would have destroyed the consul and his force in an instant on the slightest command from their captain. The reasons the consul urged might, in my husband's mind, have had some truth in them, as he represented the government of Manilla as being more jealous than even the Spanish government itself, and at last he consented that I should go on shore. This was a death-blow to me, and for an hour after hearing of the decision I was bereft of my senses; but when they came to me again, I found the three captains I have mentioned, with my husband, subdued like children. These almost strangers to me took so deep an interest in my fate, that I shall remember them with gratitude as long as my heart has a pulse to beat. They told my husband that they would protect me at all events. I was put on board the boat and carried ashore; and there being no conveyance ready to take me to Mr. Cannell's, the place which had been provided for me when I consented to stay, I was obliged to stand on the landing-place until my friends could procure one for me, subject to the gaze of every rude wretch who came there; and curiosity had collected many. From every appearance, I was fully satisfied that the consul had scattered slanders about me and my husband, in order that I might feel myself so shunned and ruined as to fly to him for protection; but I had made up my mind to die there before I would even speak to him. I was at length conveyed to Mr. Cannell's hospitable mansion, and treated with every possible kindness.

I afterward learned that Mr. Morrell came on shore that night, and not finding the head of the revenue in the city, could not get the protection and information he sought; and our friends Snow, Daggett, and Harris, fearing that blood might be spilled in the affray,—for the consul

had watched his movements, and was at the
hotel almost as soon as my husband reached
there,—interfered. The consul now assumed
another ground, which was, that the Antarctic
was showing false lights, and that her crew probably intended some mischief to the city. This
was repelled as a base and false insinuation by
all the gentlemen present. My husband's friends
thinking it better for me to remain on shore a
short time than for him to proceed to desperate
lengths, took him by main force and put him on
board his boat, taking his pledge to proceed to
sea, and giving him theirs that I should be
shielded from persecution and insult.

I was with these kind people from the 12th of
April, 1830, until the return of the Antarctic on
the 26th of June following. After my husband's
departure my story was soon known to all the
people of Manilla, and I was treated by them
with great attention; amid all their kindness,
however, I felt like one who was fifteen thousand
miles from home, lonely and distressed. My
mind was constantly agitated for my husband's
safety more than for my own. During his absence I was frequently annoyed by notes from the
consul, which I never deigned to answer. The
government became acquainted with the whole
story, and distinctly disavowed every connexion
with the transaction, or even any the slightest
knowledge of it. This gave me great satisfaction, as I then knew the extent of the consul's
villany and gross falsehood.

On the seventy-fifth day after the sailing of
the Antarctic, as I was looking with a glass from
my window, as I had done for many days previously, I saw my husband's well-known signal at

the mast-head of an approaching vessel. I communicated this intelligence to my friends, who
hastened to carry me on board. We reached the
vessel, and I was no sooner on board than I found
myself in my husband's arms; but the scene was
too much for my enfeebled frame, and I was for
some time insensible. On coming to myself, I
looked around and saw my brother, pale and ema-
ciated. My forebodings were dreadful when I
perceived that the number of the crew was sadly
reduced from what it was when I was last on
board. I dared not trust myself to make any
inquiries, and all seemed desirous to avoid explanations. I could not rest in this state of mind,
and ventured to ask what had become of the men ?
My husband, with his usual frankness, sat down
and detailed to me the whole affair, the substance
of which was as follows. I shall only state the
outlines ; his Journal will give the particulars of
the dreadful tragedy. I was in a manner prepared for the story by observing the sad looks of
the survivors, who all seemed anxious to tell the
tale, but waited for my husband to do it. At
length he mustered courage to inform me of his
melancholy disaster, in a brief and general manner, and I have not had courage at any one time
since to go over the whole of it.

It seems, that after leaving Manilla, to me the
memorable 12th of April, he discovered several
islands, the particulars of which will be found in
his Journal ; but they not affording the articles he
was in search of, he continued his voyage until
the 23d of May, when he came to six islands that
were surrounded by a coral reef. Here was a
plenty of biche-de-mer, and he made up his mind
to get a cargo of this and what shell he could procure. On the 21st, he sent a boat's crew on shore,

to clear away the brush and prepare a place to
cure the biche-de-mer. The natives now came off
to the vessel, and seemed quiet, although it was
evident that they had never seen a white man
before, and the islands bore no traces of ever
having been visited by civilized men. The people were a large, savage-looking race, but Mr.
Morrell was lulled to security by their civil and
harmless appearance, and their fondness of visiting
the vessel to exchange their fruits for trinkets
and other commodities attractive to the savages in
these climes. They were shown in perfect friendship all parts of the vessel, and appeared pleased
with the attentions paid them. The crew were
employed for several days in planting seeds in
different parts of the island, where the best soil
was found—seeds of such things as it was thought
would be useful to them. The forge and all the
blacksmith's tools were got on shore, but the
savages soon stole the greater part of them. This
was an unpropitious circumstance, but Mr. Morrell thought that he could easily recover them;
and to accomplish this, he took six of his men,
well armed, and marched directly to the village
where the king lived. This was a lovely place,
formed in a grove of trees. Here he met two
hundred warriors, all painted for battle, armed
with bows and arrows ready for an onset, waving
their war-plumes, and eager to engage. On turning round he saw nearly as many more in his
rear—it was a critical moment—the slightest fear
was sure death. Mr. Morrell addressed his com-
rades, and in a word told them that if they did
not act in concert, and in the most dauntless manner, instant death would be inevitable. He then
threw down his musket, drew his cutlass, and
holding a pistol in his right hand, he pushed for

the king, knowing in what reverence savages in general hold the person of their monarch. In an instant the pistol was at the king's breast, and the cutlass waved over his head. The savages had arrowed their bows, and were ready, at the slightest signal, to have shot a cloud of missiles at the handful of white men; but in an instant, when they saw the danger of their king, they dropped their bows to the ground. At this fortunate moment, the captain marched around the circle, and compelled those who had come with war-clubs to throw those down also; all which he ordered his men to secure and collect into a heap. The king was then conducted with several of his chiefs on board the Antarctic, and kept until next day. They were treated with every attention, but strictly guarded all night. On the following morning he gave them a good breakfast, loaded them with presents,—for which they seemed grateful, and laboured hard to convince their conqueror that they were friendly to him and his crew,—sent them ashore, together with some of his men to go on with the works which had been commenced; but feeling that a double caution was necessary, he sent a reinforcement to his men on shore, well armed. With these he sent more presents for those chiefs who had not been on board.

All were cautioned to be on their guard; but every thing was unavailing, for not long after this, a general attack was made on the men from the woods, in so sudden a manner that they were overthrown at once. Two of the crew, who were in the small boat, made their escape out of the reach of the arrows, and had the good fortune to pick up three others who had thrown themselves

c 3

into the water for safety.   On hearing the horrid
yells of the savages the whale-boat was sent with
ten men, who, with great exertions, saved two
more of the crew.   The rest all fell, at one untimely moment, victims to savage barbarity!   It
was an awful and a heart-sickening moment; fourteen of the crew had perished—they were murdered, mangled, and their corpses thrown upon
the strand without the possibility of receiving the
rites of Christian burial, rites so desirable among
all civilized nations.   Four of the survivors were
wounded—the heat was intolerable—the spirits
of the crew were broken down, and a sickness
came over their hearts that would not be con-
trolled by the power of medicine—a sickness
arising from moral causes, that would not yield to
science nor art.

In this situation, Capt. Morrell made the best
of his way for Manilla, at which port he arrived
as I have before stated.   I grew pale over the
narrative; it filled my dreams for many nights,
and occupied my thoughts for many days, I may
say, almost exclusively.   I dreaded the thought
or the mention of the deed, and yet I wished I
had been there; I might have done some good,
or if not, I might have assisted to dress the
wounded, among whom was my own dear, heroic
brother.   He received an arrow in the breast, but
his good constitution soon got over the shock,
though he was pale even when I saw him, so
many days after the event.   My husband had
now lost every thing but his courage, his honour,
and his perseverance; but the better part of the
community of Manilla had become his friends,
while the American consul was delighted, as we
heard from unquestionable authority, with our
misfortunes.   He was alone!

CHAPTER III.

Prepare for a second Voyage to Massacre Island—The Crew—
Reach Massacre Island—Contest with the Natives—The Ap-
pearance of Shaw, who was supposed to be dead—Account
of his Sufferings there—Further Hostilities with the Natives
—Description of the Means of Defence—Attack upon the
Castle—Discovery of the Remains of those murdered—Fu-
neral Honours paid them—Leaving the Place—Bread-fruit
Tree.

CAPTAIN MORRELL now petitioned the governor of Manilla for leave to take out a new crew
of seventy additional men, sixty-six of whom were
to be Manilla men, as they are commonly called,
meaning half-blood Indians, who have all the
jealousy of the Spaniard and the cunning and
ferocity of the savage. It was said that no ship
had for years dared to take more than five or six
of them on a voyage, and every one remonstrated
against taking so many; but my husband contended that their resentments in former cases
had been aroused by improper treatment, and
he would try the experiment. The men were
shipped, and the schooner ready for sea in a
short time, notwithstanding the consul made
every effort to prevent our obtaining any assistance in Manilla. But the tooth of the serpent
was broken, for he could do nothing to prevent
Messrs. Cannell and Gellis from coming forward
and advancing my husband such means as were
required to fit him out to retrace his course over
the same pathless seas, and to the same savage
lands.

On the 18th of July, 1830, the Antarctic was ready to sail again for the Massacre Islands, as my husband had named the group where he lost his men. When I went on board, I found a crew of eighty-five men, fifty-five of them savages as fierce as those we were about to encounter, and as dangerous if not properly managed. One would have thought that I should have shrunk from this assemblage as from those of Massacre Island, but I entered my cabin with a light step; I did not fear savage men half so much as I did a civilized brute. I was with my husband; he was not afraid, why should I be? This was my reasoning, and I found it safe. The schooner appeared as formidable as any thing possibly could of her size; she had great guns, ten in number, I believe, small arms, boarding pikes, cutlasses, pistols, and a great quantity of ammunition. She was a war-horse in every sense of the word but that of animal life, and that she seemed partially to have, or one would have thought so to hear the sailors talk of her. She coursed over the waters with every preparation for fight; and from experience I can say, that the more helpless we are, the more we delight in viewing all the preparations for defence.

On the 13th of September, the Antarctic again reached Massacre Island. I could only view the place as a Golgotha, and shuddered as we neared it; but I could see that most of the old crew, who came hither at the time of the massacre, were panting for revenge, although their captain had endeavoured to impress upon them the folly of gratifying such a passion, if we could gain our purpose by mildness mixed with firmness. We had no sooner made our appearance in the harbour at Massacre Island, on the 14th, than we were attacked by about three hundred warriors. We opened a brisk fire upon them, and they immediately retreated. This was the first battle I ever saw where men in anger met men in earnest. We were now perfectly safe ; our Manilla men were brave as Cæsar ; they were anxious to be landed instantly, to fight these Indians at once. They felt as much superior, no doubt, to these ignorant savages, as the philosopher does to the peasant. This the captain would not permit ; he knew his superiority while on board his vessel, and he also knew that this superiority must be, in a manner, lost to him as soon as he landed.

The firing had ceased and the enemy had retired, when a single canoe appeared coming from the shore with one man in it. We could not conjecture what this could mean. The man was as naked as a savage and as highly painted, but he managed his paddle with a different hand from the savages. When he came alongside, he spoke to us in English, and we recognised LEONARD SHAW, one of our old crew, whom we supposed among the dead. The meeting had that joyousness about it that cannot be felt in ordinary life ; he was dead and buried, and now was alive again ! We received him as one might imagine ; surprise, joy, wonder, took possession of us all, and we made him recount his adventures, which were wonderful enough.

Shaw was wounded when the others were slain ; he fled to the woods, and succeeded at that time in escaping from death. Hunger at length induced him to leave the woods and attempt to give himself up to the savages, but coming in sight of the horrid spectacle of the bodies of his friends and companions roasting for a cannibal feast, he rushed again into the woods with the intent rather to starve than to trust to such wretches for protection. For four days and nights he remained in his hiding-place, when he was forced to go in pursuit of something to keep himself from starving. After some exertion, he obtained three cocoanuts, which were so young that they did not afford much sustenance, but were sufficient to keep him alive fifteen days, during which time he suffered from the continually falling showers, which left him dripping wet. In the shade of his hiding-place he had no chance to dry himself, and on the fifteenth day he ventured to stretch himself in the sun; but he did not remain long undisturbed; an Indian saw him and gave the alarm, and he was at once surrounded by a host of the savages. The poor suffering wretch implored them to be merciful, but he implored in vain; one of them struck him on the back of the head with a war-club and laid him senseless upon the ground, and for a while left him as dead. When he recovered, and had gathered his scattered senses, he observed a chief who was not among those by whom he had been attacked, and made signs to him that he would be his slave if he would save him. The savage intimated to him to follow, which he did, and had his wound most cruelly dressed by the savage, who poured hot water into it, and filled it with sand.

As soon as the next day, while yet in agony with his wound, he was called up and set to work in making knives and other implements from the iron hoops and other plunder from the

forge when the massacre took place. This was
indeed hard, for the poor fellow was no mechanic,
though a first-rate jack tar, and had never laboured
much out of his profession ; however, necessity
made him a blacksmith, and he got along pretty
well.

The savages were not yet satisfied, and they
made him march five or six miles to visit a
distinguished chief. This was done in a state
of nudity, without any thing like sandals or
moccasins to protect his feet from the flint-stones
and sharp shells, and under the burning rays
of an intolerable sun. Blood marked his foot-
steps. The king met him, and compelled him to
debase himself by the most abject ceremonies
of slavery. He was now overcome, and with a
dogged indifference was ready to die. He could
not, he would not walk back ; his feet were
lacerated, swollen, and almost in a state of putre-
faction. The savages saw this, and took him
back by water, but only to experience new tor-
ments. The young ones imitated their elders,
and these graceless little rascals pulled out his
beard and whiskers, and eyebrows and eyelashes.
In order to save himself some part of the pain
of this wretched process of their amusement, he
was permitted to perform a part of this work with
his own hands !   He was indeed a pitiable object,
but one cannot die when one wishes, and be
guiltless. This was not all he suffered ; he was
almost starved to death, for they gave him only
the offal of the fish they caught, and this but
sparingly ; he sustained himself by catching rats,
and these offensive creatures were his principal
food for a long time. He understood that the
natives did not suffer the rats to be killed, and
therefore he had to do it secretly in the night-time.

Thus passed the days of the prisoner ; the head
of the poor fellow not yet healed, notwithstanding
all his efforts to get the sand out of his wound,
until a short time before his deliverance, when it
was made known to him that he was to be immo-
lated for a feast to the king of the group! All
things had now become matters of indifference
to him, and he heard the horrid story with great
composure. All the preparations for the sacrifice
were got up in his presence, near the very spot
where the accursed feast of sculls had been held.
All was in readiness, and waited a long time for
the king ; but he did not come, and the ceremony
was put off. Shaw has often expressed himself
fully on this subject, and said that he could not
but feel some regret that his woes were not to be
finished, as there was no hope for him, and to
linger always in this state of agitation was worse
than death ; but mortals are short-sighted, for he
was destined to be saved through the instrumen-
tality of his friends.

His soul was again agitated by hope and fear,
in the extremes, on the day when the Antarctic
made her appearance a second time on the coast.
He feared that her arrival would be the signal for
his destruction ; but if this should not happen,
might he not be saved ? The whole population
of the island he was on, and those of the others
of the group, manned their war-canoes for a formidable attack, and the fate of the prisoner was
suspended for a season. The attack was commenced by the warriors in the canoes, without
doubt confident of success ; but the well-directed
fire from the Antarctic soon repulsed them, and
they sought the shore in paroxysms of rage,
which was changed to fear when they found that

the big guns of the schooner threw their shot directly into the village, and were rapidly demolishing their dwellings. It was in this state of fear and humility that Shaw was sent off to the vessel to stop the carnage and destruction; they were glad to have peace on any terms. They now gave up their boldness, and as it was the wish of all but the Manilla men to spare the effusion of human blood, it was done as soon as safety would admit of it.

The story of Shaw's sufferings raised the indignation of every one of the Americans and English we had on board, and they were violently desirous to be led on to attack the whole of Massacre Island, and extirpate the race at once. They felt at this moment as if it would be an easy thing to kill the whole of them; but Capt. Morrell was not to be governed by any impulse of passion—he had other duties to perform; yet he did not reprimand the men for this feeling, thinking it might be of service to him hereafter.

After taking every precaution to secure safety, by getting up his boarding nettings many feet above the deck, and every thing prepared for defence or attack, the frame of a house, brought for the purpose, was got up on a small uninhabited island,—which had been purchased of the king in exchange for useful articles, such as axes, shaves, and other mechanical tools, precisely such as the Indians wished for. The captain landed with a large force, and began to fell the trees to make a castle for defence. Finding two large trees, nearly six feet through, he prepared the limbs about forty feet from the ground, and raised a platform extending from one to the other, with an arrow-proof bulwark around it. Upon this platform were stationed a garrison of twenty men, with four brass swivels. This platform was covered with a water-tight roof, and the men slept there at night upon their arms, to keep the natives from approaching to injure the trees or fort by fire, the only way they could assail the garrison. It looked indeed like a castle—formidable in every respect; and the ascent to it was by a ladder, which was drawn up at night into the warlike habitation. The next step was to clear the woods from around the castle, in order to prevent a lurking enemy from coming within arrow-shot of the fort. Next the house was raised, and made quite a fine appearance, being one hundred and fifty feet long, forty feet broad, and very high. The castle protected the house and the workmen in it, and both house and castle were so near the sea-board that the Antarctic, while riding at anchor, protected both. The castle was well stocked with provisions in case of a siege.

The next day, after all was in order for business, a large number of canoes made their appearance near Massacre Island. Shaw said that this fleet belonged to another island, and he had never known them to stop there before. My husband, having some suspicions, did not suffer the crew to go ashore the next morning at the usual time; and about eight o'clock one of the chiefs came off, as usual, to offer us fruits, but no boat was sent to meet him. He waited some time for us and then directed his course to our island, which my husband had named Wallace Island, in memory of the officer who had bravely fallen in fight on the day of the massacre. This was surprising, as not a single native had set a foot on that island since our works were begun; but we were not kept long in suspense, for we saw about a hundred war-canoes start from the back side of Massacre Island and make towards Wallace Island. We knew that war was their object, and the Antarctic was prepared for battle. The chief who came to sell us fruits, landed in front of the castle, the first man. He gave the warhoop, and about two hundred warriors, who had concealed themselves in the woods during the darkness of the night, rushed forward. The castle was attacked on both sides, and the Indians discharged their arrows at the building in the air, till they were stuck, like porcupine's quills, in every part of the roof. The garrison was firm, and waited in silence until the assailants were within a short distance, when they opened a tremendous fire from their swivels, loaded with canister shot; the men were ready with their muskets also, and the Antarctic opened her fire of large guns, all with a direct and deadly aim at the leaders of the savage band. The execution was very great, and in a short time the enemy made a precipitate retreat, taking with them their wounded and as many of their dead as they could. The ground was strewed with implements of war, which the savages had thrown away in their flight, or which had belonged to the slain. The enemy did not expect such a reception, and they were prodigiously frightened; the sound of the cannon alarmed every woman and child in the group as it echoed through the forest or died upon the wave; they had never heard such a roar before, for in our first fight there was no necessity for such energy. The Indians took to the water, leaving only a few in their canoes, to get them off, while the garrison hoisted the American flag, and were greeted by

those on board of the schooner, who were in high
spirits at their victory, which was achieved without the loss of a man on our part, and only two
wounded. The music struck up " Yankee Doodle," " Rule Britannia," &c., and the crew could
hardly restrain their joy to think they had beaten
their enemy so easily.

The boats were all manned, and most of the
crew went on shore to mark the devastation
which had been made. I saw all this without
any sensation of fear, so easy is it for a woman
to catch the spirit of those near her. If I had, a
few months before this time, read of such a battle,
I should have trembled at the detail of the incidents ; but seeing all the animation and courage
which were displayed, and noticing, at the same
time, how coolly all was done, every particle of
fear left me, and I stood quite as collected as any
heroine of former days. Still I could not but
deplore the sacrifice of the poor, misguided, ignorant creatures, who wore the human form, and had
souls to save. Must the ignorant always be
taught civilization through blood ?—situated as
we were, no other course could be taken.

We now went on finishing our house and
clearing more of the woods. Our wounded were
taken on board, and had their wounds dressed :
they were not of an alarming nature, although
at first we were apprehensive that the arrows
might have been poisoned ; but they were not,
and the men soon recovered.

On the morning of the 19th, to our great surprise, the chief who had previously come out to
bring us fruit, and had done so on the morning
of our great battle, came again in his canoe and
called for Shaw, on the edge of the reef, with his

usual air of kindness and friendship, offering fruit, and intimating a desire for trade, as though nothing had happened. The offer seemed fair, but all believed him to be treacherous. The small boat was sent to meet him, but Shaw, who we feared was now an object of vengeance, was not sent in her. She was armed for fear of the worst, and the cockswain of the boat had orders to kill the chief if he should discover any treachery in him. As our boat came alongside the canoe, the crew saw a bearded arrow attached to a bow ready for the purpose of revenge. Just as the savage was about to bend his bow, the cockswain levelled his piece, and shot the traitor through the body; his wound was mortal, but he did not expire immediately. At this instant a fleet of canoes made their appearance to protect their chief. The small boat lost one of her oars in the fight, and we were obliged to man two large boats and send them to the place of contest. The large boats were armed with swivels and muskets, and a furious engagement ensued. The natives were driven from the water, but succeeded in taking off their wounded chief, who expired as he reached the shore.

After the death of *Hennean*, the name of the chief we had slain, the inhabitants of Massacre Island fled to some other place, and left all things as they were before our attack upon them, and our men roamed over it at will. The sculls of several of our slaughtered men were found at Hennean's door, trophies of his bloody prowess. These were now buried with the honours of war; the colours of the Antarctic were lowered half-mast, minute-guns were fired, and dirges were played by our band, in honour of those who had fallen untimely on Massacre Island. This was all that feeling or affection could bestow. Those so inhumanly murdered had at last the rites of burial performed for them : millions have perished without such honours. It seems to be a passion of every age and nation, of every religious creed under the sun, to have funeral rites performed over their dead bodies. This love of posthumous honours is deeply ingrafted into our systems, if it is not implanted there by nature : it is the last sad office that can be paid; and though last, not least.

We now commenced collecting and curing biche-de-mer, and should have succeeded to our wishes, if we had not been continually harassed by the natives as soon as we began our efforts. We continued to work in this way until the 28th of October, when we found that the natives were still hostile, and on that day one of our men was attacked on Massacre Island, but escaped death through great presence of mind, and shot the brother of the chief Hennean ; this man's name was THOMAS HOLMES, a cool, deliberate English-man. Such an instance of self-possession, in such great danger as that in which he was placed, would have given immortality to a greater man. We felt ourselves much harassed and vexed by the persevering savages, and finding it impossible to make them understand our motives and inten-tions, we came to the conclusion to leave the place forthwith. This was painful, after such struggles and sacrifices and misfortunes; but there was no other course to pursue. Accordingly, on the 3d of November, 1830, we set fire to our house and castle, and departed by the light of them, taking the biche-de-mer we had collected and cured. If we had been left to pursue our course without molestation, there can be no doubt but that a fine voyage would have been made; for in no place is the article better or more abundant.

We left this place for Bouka Island, where we soon arrived. The manners and customs of the people here are the same as those at the Massacre Islands; but they have more formidable canoes, of better construction, and they move swifter through the water. It is not a little surprising, that in such a short distance, better canoes—the whole of their ingenuity in ship-building—should be found than at the Massacre Islands. Between these islands we found large quantities of sperm-whale, as tame as kittens; probably no harpoon had ever been thrown at them since the art of whaling has been known. All on board thought that at certain seasons this might be good whaling ground; but those who visit these seas must be cautious how they expose themselves for an instant, as the savages are so powerful and treacherous. This island abounds in biche-de-mer and sandal-wood; and if these people could be trusted, a good voyage, it is thought, could be made here.

Nature, the kind mother and nurse to all her children, seems to have been very provident to these islanders of the Southern as well as to those of the Western Pacific, particularly in giving them the bread-fruit tree, as it is called by Europeans. It grows wild on almost all the islands of the Pacific, within thirty degrees of the equator, but is in perfection from the tenth to the twentieth. It is a tall tree, about fifty feet in height, with spreading branches and large leaves, and makes

an excellent shelter in the heat of the day. It
bears fruit for three-quarters of the year in most
places, and near the equator longer than that
time. The bread-fruit is a large round fruit, about
as big as a common ostrich's egg. The pulp is
the only part eaten, and this not raw. The fruit
is generally cut into several pieces, wrapped up
in an envelope of the leaf of the same tree, and
put into ground which has been heated, or among
embers, and there made to roast for half an hour.
It has the appearance of the potato, with a slight
taste of the tomato. These cooks of nature understand mixing with this roasted fruit the milk
of the cocoanut and a great many other vegetables, all of which it is impossible distinctly to understand, either from seeing them prepare it, or
from their description of the preparation. The
same quantity of this food is more nutritious than
either the plantain or bananas alone, and much
preferred by the natives. A few trees supply a
family; but these are not all the uses of this tree.
The inner bark is fibrous, and of this some of
the natives make cloth, fishing-lines, &c., and the
wood is good for making canoes. The wood is
as soft, or softer than our white-pine or bass, when
green, but grows hard by being thoroughly sea-
soned. It is not easily corrupted; like the syca-
more, it will last many years without decaying.
This tree has been brought from the Pacific to
the West Indies, and flourishes well there; but
the Africans in slavery lose their taste for natural
food in a great measure, and prefer the maize to
bread-fruit, and of course the cultivation of it is
not much encouraged

CHAPTER IV.

St. George's Channel—Beauty of the Scenery—Birds of New-Britain—Natural Society—Warlike Instruments of the Natives—Island of Papua—Birds of Paradise—Volcanic Islands—New Discoveries—Hostilities of the Natives—Productions of these Islands—Ambergris—Return to Manilla.

WE now shaped our course for New-Ireland, and continued our way through St. George's Channel, which is formed by the west side of New-Ireland and the east side of New-Britain. This channel is safe, or it seemed so to us at least, and has been described as one of the most beautiful on the globe ; and I think it is. The hills on each side are lofty, and the descent to the sea is gentle and regular. The forests are of the most massy growth, and greatly diversified by various kinds of trees, intermingled with luxuriant flowers and fruit trees. The air, as you sail along in a fine day, is aromatic with the nutmeg and other spicy groves. These islands are said to be not only abounding in the productions of nature, but capable of raising almost every thing in the known world. The biche-de-mer, hawksbill tortoise-shell, red coral, ambergris, and no doubt many other things, are found here, such as pearl-shell and sandal-wood; for it seems to be a law of nature, that where she shows her kindnesses she outpours them in great abundance. The natives visited us, bringing plenty of fruits and fowls, which we purchased for a few pieces

D

of iron hoops and some trinkets. Few people that I have seen are better formed than these islanders; they are dark, stout built, and are susceptible of becoming the most civilized in the Eastern world, I should think. In the course of the day we had ample opportunity to from an opinion of them; and after a short time one gets into a habit of forming more correct opinions in an hour than could be made up in a day, when first launched into a world of wonders.

We landed on New-Britain, and found a great variety of birds, some of beautiful plumage, and others of most melodious notes. Hogs and dogs are also found here, and are plentiful to a great extent. The fish are remarkably fine around the island. In fine, these people seemed to me to be the happiest of all the race of wild men I had ever seen. It is amusing to think how soon we become enamoured with the thought of natural society, and in moments of contemplation wish to be found among people of a primitive cast. The thousand evils of social life crowd upon us when we look at these forests and their inhabitants; there is no vulgar wretchedness, as seen in crowded cities—no squalid diseases; there is nothing of aristocratic contumely, and the laws of nature are only slightly regulated by convention or necessity.

From here we sailed to examine the north cape of New-Britain. We were visited by the inhabitants, who seemed of a much more savage nature than those of New-Ireland. The shores are surrounded with coral reefs, about eight or ten miles from them. Arrowsmith's charts, my husband said, were pretty correct; but he regretted very much that he could not spare time to give a more correct one. It is wonderful to me that they are so correct as we find them, so little time could be bestowed upon the subject. We continued to keep near the shore for some time, having now and then a little difficulty with the natives; for they thought our vessel so small that a crew of one or two canoes would take her with ease; we had only to splash the water about them, however, with a cannot shot or two, to make them keep at a fearful distance. There is something terrible to a savage ear in the sound of big guns, and I know not whose ear ever gets familiar to the roar of a full-mouthed battery. I must confess, though I thought myself quite brave, that I always trembled a little to hear a great gun fired, and to feel the tremulous motion of the ship at its recoil. Fortunately we were not obliged to sacrifice any of the natives for our safety, as we could get along without proceeding to such extremities. Half the blood that has been spilt in the world might have been avoided by prudence and moral reflection. The natives often act from ignorance, and a natural love of gain or power; and the civilized man turns his rage upon the poor wretches, as if they were as able to reason as an enlightened European. If we had a hold on their affections, I have no doubt that we should find them strong and permanent; for they have but few conventional reasons to break in upon a course of nature, and as far as I have watched the operations of nature, the savage loves his offspring as much as civilized man. But it is in vain to moralize, for this will not change habits, manners, or morals. Oh! for that blessed day when civilization, attended by all the Christian virtues, shall reach the isles of the sea, and make glad all the nations of the earth. I am no enthusiast; but when I see what has been done at New-Zealand, I do not despair, in my time, of hearing that these very places I have attempted faintly to describe have felt the benign influences of our holy religion.

We crossed the straits, and came close under the northern shore of an island, which lies nearly in the centre of the strait. It is of some size, and my husband called it Dampier's Island, in honour of the discoverer of it. The natives came off to see us, and were very cautious; but by coaxing them with the show of trinkets, we got them alongside. While with us, they discovered more than ordinary curiosity, for savages; they examined every thing about the vessel, were curious to know the uses of the chain cables and anchors, the great guns, and every thing on board. They offered us various articles, which we purchased, such as fishing gear, spears, war-clubs, and pearl-shells; as also some of their household implements, such as knives and other instruments made of pearl-shell, and of no ordinary workmanship. They presented us some elegant spears, with pearl-shell heads, and ornamented in fine style with carving and feathers of the birds of paradise. The wooden part of these spears is of excellent heavy dark wood, resembling ebony; and the carving upon them is often really curious, and bespeaks an advance in the arts hardly believed to exist in savage life. It would not be saying enough to call them ingenious; they are tasteful. It is astonishing to those who think all barbarous nations are only on an equality, in the arts, with our North American Indians, to witness such specimens of skill in carving and ornamenting their works of war, or of taste. The villages of these islanders are laid out upon the sides of the hills, and their dwellings are shaded by the lofty cocoanut and bread-fruit trees. They seem to live happily among themselves, and to enjoy every hour of their existence; and as far as I am able to judge, the extent of human life is as great in these climates as in any part of the world. I saw no victims of disease, nor any instances of decrepitude.

On the 12th of November we left Dampier's Island, with fair weather and a fine breeze. We sailed at the rate of thirteen miles an hour, assisted by the current, and soon reached the north of Long Island, which is less elevated than the one we had just left. We saw only a few wigwams along the shore, and some natives; but we could not conveniently land, and kept on our course until we had passed the western end of Long Island, and thence proceeded to the coast of New-Guinea.

All these seas are dangerous, by reason of the coral reefs, and navigators should be on their guard, as they are liable to be suddenly run upon. The mariner is not much assisted by soundings, for these reefs arise from deep water, thrown up by volcanic power, and come from the depths of the ocean.

We now reached De Kay's Bay, the entrance to which is in latitude 5° 39′ south, and longitude 146° 2′ east. The villages around these shores are numerous and pleasant. The natives have the negro cast of features, and they are shrewd, although their appearance is as savage as well could be. They are not in person like the negro, for they are well formed in their limbs;

but no one, on looking at them, could confide in
them for an instant. Their instruments of war
make them formidable. They are expert in the
use of the bow, and send their arrows with great
directness and force. They are extremely adroit
in catching fish, which is a considerable part
of their employment.

The heads of the natives are decorated with
the plumage of the bird of paradise, of many
species. We saw many flocks of these birds
soaring high above the water; they float along
as a tuft of feathers. They are of all sizes, from
that of a pigeon to the diminutive form of a
sparrow. The noise they make in the air is not
at all melodious; it is a sort of chattering, without a distinct note. They look splendid in the
sun, and some of the most diminutive are not
the least beautiful. Fancy has given these birds
properties which nature never did; but nothing
can look more beautiful than they do when
floating along with all the colours of the rainbow
in the rays of the sun. They have such an
abundance of feathers compared to their corporeal
weight, that it is easy for them to keep on the
wing; and therefore the fabulist and romantic
have made them live for ever in flight; but
reason and examination have proved this false.
It is certain, I believe, that they flourish only near
the equator, and cannot endure the slightest chill.
They live among flowers and sandal-wood. Delicate things of nature are generally grouped
together.

The race of men, however, must make an exception to this rule. Whatever pride may say,
or think, the beauties of nature in the wilds of the
world were made without any regard to proud

man, for nature often revels in beauties, and unveils her charms to the most ecstatic extent, where man is ignorant and savage ; and man is often greatest where nature is steril and iron-bound. No bird of paradise ever spread his wings on the hills of North America, or on the mountains of Switzerland or Scotland, where man has reached the highest moral and intellectual perfection. And even when civilized man takes possession of the bowers of Eden, he does not suffer the original features of nature to remain, but sacrifices every grace and beauty to the rigid laws of utility and productiveness. The most lovely streams in our own country, adorned with dashing falls and pure water, are not suffered to run on in their natural course, but are stopped and tortured to turn a mill-wheel, or dammed up to move off obliquely and fill a canal. The aborigines look with pity on these tasteless occupants of their soil, and sigh to think that power and prosperity do not suffer the lovely face of nature to remain as it was in the days of their fathers. But utility should be paramount to taste in a world whose object is gain.

On Saturday, the 13th of November, we kept the mainland close on board of us, being obliged to sheer off sometimes to clear the coral reefs. In the afternoon we were close to a headland that seemed hanging over the sea. Between this and the seashore, however, there were many huts of the natives in the midst of beautiful groves of cocoanut-trees. My husband told me to put the name of this cape, which is in latitude 4° 59 south, and longitude 145° 16′ east, in my journal as Cape Livingston, in honour of Edward Livingston, Esq., Secretary of State.

About six leagues from the cape, N.N.E., lies a
small volcanic island. At night the prospect was
indeed sublime; the flames were bursting from
the crater, and ascending much higher than those
of Ætna or Vesuvius, as those bursts of smoke
and fire have been described to us. The flames
reached at least, as I had been taught to measure
distances with my eye since I had been on the
voyage, a thousand feet in height. It was as
light as if ten thousand lamps were suspended
over our deck; and the stones cast up appeared
like myriads of red-hot shot thrown in the night
at incalculable distances. I gazed on this scene
as one of wonderful sublimity, and thought how
impotent language was to convey a full and com-
petent idea of it. The next day, following the
course of the island of Papua, we passed six other
volcanic islands, all of which were in full blast.

What a scene for the poet! If those of antiquity roused all their energies and exhausted
their powers of language on Ætna, whose fires
were almost burnt out when they wrote, how
would they have communicated to the world
their impressions of these numerous mountains
of infernal smoke and fire, which seemed, as it
were, in the first stage of their wrath! How
small seems the power of man, when we contemplate these wonders of nature, and ask for what
uses they were formed! After the wonder has
passed over us, we begin to see their uses; they
are the engines of the Almighty in planting
islands in the midst of the seas. By volcanic
power masses of the bottom of the ocean are
thrown up, the lava is spread abroad to a greater
or less extent, and on its surface a soil is formed;
and by some inscrutable law of nature trees grow

up, birds and animals are found upon it, and man, self-wise man, wonders and puzzles his head to tell why all this is, and makes a thousand fanciful conjectures upon what he calls the philosophy of the matter, and talks learnedly upon the nature of things. But after all, he knows but little about it. Although in our common course of life, in the midst of society, we know, when we reason, that God is everywhere, yet we see so much of the works of man that there is a sort of belief in our minds that man has much to do with all affairs in this world, and seems to divide the empire of it with its Creator. But on the widespread ocean, where nature is every thing, and man nothing, we enter, as it were, the depths of Omnipotence, and adore his majesty and power as the Being who said, and still says, in the burning mountain as in the burning bush, I AM that I AM; and who is there then that would not turn aside to see this great sight?

My husband named this promontory Woodbury's Cape, in honour of the then Chairman of Naval affairs in Congress, now Secretary of the Navy of the United States. Five miles from the cape is a fine spacious harbour, of sufficient depth of water between the rocks, but the course is narrow and winding.

The next day, November 15th, we passed another headland, which was called Cape Decatur, in honour of Capt. Stephen Decatur, formerly of the United States' navy. This day and the following we were visited by many of the natives, but were cautious of them, as we had suffered so much from their treachery.

We fell in with numerous islands, but I do not recollect that my husband gave them a name, or

D 3

that they had already had one given them. They
lie low, and are surrounded by a coral reef. Here
there is plenty of biche-de-mer, pearls, tortoise, and
oysters. Of this place I had neither latitude nor
longitude given me, and I have never inquired
the cause, but I could easily conjecture it. From
these islands the natives came off to us in great
numbers in large canoes. They made an attempt
to get us on the coral reef, by making their canoes
fast to the schooner and paddling towards the
shore ; but the wind being brisk, they could not
make any headway. Their lines soon parted,
and in their rage they shot their arrows at the
schooner. A few guns were fired over their heads
to frighten them, and make them understand the
power of those they attempted to assail. The re-
port of the cannon astounded them, and many
leaped into the sea for safety. We had already
had enough of blood, and were unwilling to shed
it. A boat was lowered while they were in confusion, and one of the natives picked up. We
took him for the purpose of educating him, by
giving him an opportunity of seeing civilization,
and then returning him to his native country.
After we had taken our prisoner, they made the
best of their way to the shore. These islands
are all thickly wooded ; the cocoanut-trees are
lofty and fruitful, and as large as any I ever saw,
and bread-fruit trees are in great profusion. The
natives dress with coral necklaces, feathers in
their hair, and numerous other ornaments, which
give them quite a stylish appearance. Tortoise-
shell and mother-of-pearl are profuse in these
ornaments, and they bear marks of opulence in all
those things which we think of importance.
Their dress is nothing more than an apron about
their loins, formed of several kinds of materials,

as they can afford, according to their rank. These natives are well formed and muscular, and their features are manly ; they are unlike any other tribe in these seas. There are one or two passages through the reefs, and after getting within them you find good anchorage.

While here, my husband purchased several pieces of *ambergris* of the natives. I examined this wonderful substance very attentively. Its colour is a darkish yellow, resembling very closely a mass of bees-wax. It had insects and beaks of birds in it, and burned very clear, as much so as bees-wax. When rubbed, it emits a perfume generally much admired. It was taken from the water, on which it was floating, about one-third of it above the surface. Numerous accounts have been given of its nature and origin. It has been said that it grows in the intestines of the sperma-ceti whale. It is true that it is often found in the whale, but generally in those that are poor and unhealthy. The whalers, I find, have a general impression that it originates there from the feeding of the whale on certain fish called squids. The orientals, however, had no such idea of its origin ; they considered it as a sea mushroom, which, growing on the bottom of the sea, was by time or accident rooted up, and coming to the surface grew harder by partial exposure to the sun. Others say that it grows on the rocks, and is washed off in storms and driven near the islands, where it is picked up by the natives. Some suppose it is wax, or a honey-comb, which, by dropping into the sea, undergoes a chymical change ; while some contend that it is a bituminous matter, that comes from the bottom of the sea. There are not a few who think that it is the

excrement of certain fish ; but the poets of the
East say that it is a gum from the tears of certain
consecrated sea-birds.

> " Around thee shall glisten the loveliest *amber*
> That ever the sorrowing sea-bird hath wept,
> And many a shell in whose hollow-wreathed chamber
> We Peris of ocean by moonlight have slept."

Whatever may be its origin or creation, it certainly has for many centuries been held in high
estimation as a perfume and for ornaments, and
its use has generally been confined to the rich and
powerful. Large pieces of it have lately been
found, and when we consider the purposes for
which it has been used,—particularly as a perfume,—the price of it is astonishing. My husband, who has been much in these seas, and often
made it a matter of traffic, is of opinion that the
natives of these islands have a correct idea of the
substance ; viz. that it is made by an insect at the
bottom of the sea, and accumulates for years ; and
that sea-birds devour it when within their reach,
which accounts for their bills being found in it.
The birds, being attracted by its glutinous qualities,
strike their beaks too deep to extricate themselves,
and their bodies decay, while the bony parts of
their beaks remain. The sperm-whale is a raven-
ous animal, and he may root it up and swallow it :
and this, perhaps, is one mode by which the God
of nature intended that the leviathan of the ocean
should be destroyed. That it is formed in the
whale seems unnatural in many respects ; the
places, too, where it is found in the most abundance, do not abound in sperm-whales, and I have
never read that it was found in any other kinds
of whales.

There is no accounting for the arbitrary laws of fashion; once a man of fashion in England, and in most cities on the Continent, must have an amber-headed cane, if he carried one at all. Gay, in his Trivia, alludes to this matter of fashion :—

" If the strong cane support thy walking hand,
Chairmen no longer shall the wall command ;
Even sturdy carmen shall thy nod obey,
And rattling coaches stop to make thee way.
This shall direct thy cautious tread aright,
Though not one glaring lamp enliven night.
Let beaux their canes, with *amber tipp'd*, produce,
Be theirs for empty show, but thine for use."

Since the days of the rage for tulips in Holland, and their high prices, there has not been a more decidedly mere creature of fashionable imagination than that of a partiality among the rich for amber, whether dug from the mines, or found in another form floating upon the water, or torn from the murdered whale. It is, perhaps, the only way that commerce can be sustained, to supply the whims of the opulent as well as the honest wants of the community : the artificial wants of society support a great proportion of the people of every country.

We left these islands with a fine breeze, and soon found ourselves near another one, low and uninhabited, and within a coral reef. Not far from this we discovered another island not laid down on any chart we had on board. Here we were visited by the natives, and found them, like most of these aborigines, dangerous to deal with. These groups are thinly inhabited. I am fully of opinion that numerous islands, containing articles of valuable commerce, are still to be found

in these seas ; it cannot be that half of them are
yet discovered.

On the 26th of November we took the trade-
winds in latitude 6° 0', and longitude 144° 55',
and between this and New-Britain we discovered
the islands from which we took two natives,
whom my husband named SUNDAY and MONDAY.
On the 27th we crossed a coral reef of several
miles in circumference, with from three to ten
fathoms of water on it.   From hence we steered
for the St. Bernardino, which we entered on the
9th of December, and the next day touched at
Port of Santa Sinto, and took in a supply of provisions, of which we were in great want, as we
had been on short allowance for many days, which
I feared would create some disturbance on board ;
but when the sailors and Manilla men saw that,
we in the cabin were on allowance also, they
were kept quiet as lambs—so easy is it to govern
others when we can govern ourselves.   During
our whole cruise from Manilla we had no sickness, or none to speak of,—one man only requiring
medicine.   This was effected, in these warm and
often sickly climes, by keeping all in a state of
cleanliness, without the use of ardent spirits, and
never suffering the crew, in any case, to be long
idle.   Vinegar is an excellent thing for keeping a
vessel sweet, and we used it freely.

We now made the best of our way to Manilla,
and reached there on Thursday, the 14th of December, after an absence of about six months.
The crew had behaved well, no punishment having been required during the whole voyage.   All
were treated well, and all behaved well ; I went
to sleep as quietly as if I had been in my native

city, and was, in fact, as secure ; so much is there in a spirit of government. I have sometimes thought that tigers and lions might be tamed, if they were perfectly governed. On our arrival at Manilla, as I apprehended, we found that our evils were not at an end. Our English and Spanish friends were as kind as people could be ; still the consul continued his persecutions.

CHAPTER V.

AFTER staying here nearly a month, we were
ready, and sailed on the 13th of January, 1831.
It was hard parting with some of our friends,
who had been so kind to us in our difficulties.
Every heart responds to the old adage, "a friend
in need is a friend indeed;" and distance from
home, too, enhances every kindness, as it re-
doubles every insult. I have found friends fifteen
thousand miles from my native land, and these
among strangers; while our troubles came from
one of our own countrymen. Our government
should be cautious what sort of men they send
abroad; the people among whom they reside
judge the whole nation from its representatives.
I know this is not correct; but they will so reason
in most cases, and it is natural that they should.
For my own part, I expected friendship from my
countrymen wherever they were to be met with

abroad, and I hope no one has been so unfortunate as I have.   But I have said enough upon
this subject, perhaps too much ; yet it pressed so
grievously upon my heart that I could not be
silent, and feel satisfied.   I wished the world to
know my sufferings ; their recital may serve a
good purpose by putting others on their guard.

While in Manilla I visited several churches and
one of the convents.   The churches are like those
of Old Spain, built about three centuries ago.
The light in these gothic temples is softened, and
the whole appearance is that of solemn grandeur.
To a Protestant there seems to be too much pomp
and circumstance in the Catholic worship ; but
if one can get rid of this impression upon his
mind, the ceremonies are imposing.   The Scripture pieces that ornament these churches are not
so numerous as I expected to find them, but some
of them are said to be from the hands of the
great masters of Italy and Spain.   I was at first
inclined to think that paintings in churches were
out of place, however solemn and scriptural the
subjects ; but I soon became pleased with examining them as works of art, and at times thought
they made wholesome impressions on my mind
in moments of devotion.   These large paintings
look better while the organ, with its swelling
peals, is raising the soul to heaven by the divinity
of music.

I must confess, too, that my impressions of a
convent were not quite correct.   I had only
known them as represented in novels, the prison-
houses of beautiful girls, thrust there by proud
or hard-hearted parents, never to catch a glimpse
of the world except through a grate of iron.
My visits to this cloister convinced me of one

thing I never dreamed of before; which was, that a woman may be a nun, even if she be old and ugly too. A great proportion of the women that I saw in this convent were solemn, staid, and old: now and then a young and handsome girl was seen among them; but then she bore no marks of misery about her, but seemed composed, softened, and meditative, without any haggardness from weeping her soul away. They all seemed full of occupation; some were making clothes for the poor, while others were engaged in embroidering and painting. Every thing that came from their hands had a nicety and delicacy about it as if wrought by fairy fingers. There is no idleness in these convents, as is generally supposed; their devotions begin at the dawn of the day, and are often repeated during the whole of it, or until late in the evening, in some form or other. But after all, their lives are not more monotonous than that of most women in many parts of the world, where all the change in their lives, except such as age makes, as the Vicar of Wakefield says, is from the blue bed to the brown. The Spanish women are well formed, though not possessing that extreme delicacy and refinement which are often, in our own country, considered as being necessary to exquisite beauty. They have no small share of health and strength in their beauty; nor can their complexions be compared with the English or American ladies for whiteness and brilliancy; but there is a warmth of colouring in them that gives a sweet animation to their countenances, whenever they are engaged in conversation; and no eye can be finer than that of the Spanish lady's. They are kind-hearted, and if ever vindictive, as they are repretented to be, it is from "love to hatred turned" by some insult or neglect. The Spanish ladies are not wanting in high heroic bravery; I can readily believe all that was said of their heroism at Saragossa. They love liberty and independence, in their own way, as much as any women I know of. They dress well, in their own style; their clothes are rich and splendid, but they do not affect the French or English fashions. I have seen some most splendid dresses at a ball given by the governor's lady; and there is a fine elastic step in the dance of the Spanish lady which is at once graceful, modest, and elegant.

Some of the Spanish at Manilla are as near the days of Philip II. in their manners and customs as some of our Canadian friends are to those of Louis XIV. There is the Moorish loftiness often seen among those in humble stations; and the Spaniard is a good subject. He is loyal to his king, shows no restlessness, lives frugally, and is content with what he has. He is quick and sensitive, but neither captious nor quarrelsome in his general intercourse with society; but terrible in his resentments from wounded honour. The stories of gallantries and assassinations are now and then true, but there have not been a hundredth part so many of these things as have been represented by the English and the French. England, from the days of Queen Mary, has had no good-will towards Spain; and since her time, there has been no connexion by marriage between the royal families of these kingdoms. England, on becoming Protestant, was obliged to seek alliances in Protestant Germany, and there had been no real friendship between these nations from the divorce of Catharine to the time when England fought France in Spain, under Sir John Moore and others; and then it was rather a union of purpose than of feeling. Spain had been plundered by French and English bucaniers, from 1660 to 1730, and the two nations took no great pains to extirpate this formidable race of freebooters, until they began to rob and plunder their own ships. Almost every thing we have had of the history of the Spaniards has come through English writers.

As far as I could judge, the style of ordinary conversation is less familiar and colloquial among the Spaniards than among us. Some of the ladies in Manilla, from having Chinese domestics, have become in some measure acquainted with the Chinese language, and made some proficiency in writing it. They say that no people abound more in romantic tales than the Chinese; that even the common people, who have but little erudition, have numerous tales of wonder to communicate for the pleasure of the circle to which they belong. I believe every nation has its region of fiction and story-tellers, except our own, and we began our national existence with too much accurate knowledge to be under the necessity of having recourse to fiction. The Tartars have less refinement than the Chinese, but as much force of character, with less industry and economy. The distinguishing traits of character between the two nations, although they are ranked with each other, are prominent, both physically and morally.

During my residence in Manilla I witnessed one of those terrors of nations, an earthquake. I was not so much alarmed as I thought I should be. Courage is a virtue which is generally ac-

quired by the necessity of braving dangers; and
after the dread of storms and sickness at sea, I
did not feel much alarmed at other things, even
such as would, if they had overtaken me before
my voyage, have shaken me like a leaf. The
first thing that struck me was the appearance
of people in the street kneeling and saying their
prayers wherever they could see a crucifix, or
an image of the Blessed Virgin. The Chinese
was looking around with his little twinkling eye,
half-amazed, yet unwilling to retire from the
scene of business while any remained to buy or
sell. The Christians were seen flocking to the
churches, where mass was being celebrated; men,
women, and children hurried to prostrate themselves before the altar, thinking that the prayers
of the clergyman could avert the Divine decree.
I went with my English friends to visit the
churches, which were full to overflowing, all
prostrate before their favourite saint, imploring
him or her to interfere with the Saviour to assist
them. It was a solemn scene; the sobs and
sighs broke upon the ear, and were indeed distressing. From the convents could be heard a low
and solemn chant, and then it died away again.
There was not a word of courtesy spoken in the
streets, except what passed between the English
and American people. As yet there was no noise
or rumbling, but a frightful stillness in the air;
the birds were silent, and the whole animal
world seemed to partake of the terror. The
fishing families took to their boats, but I could
not see a single line thrown out for fish; they
made the most melancholy spectacle of all. At
first there was no motion of the water; it wore
the glassy surface that seemed immoveable. At

length a gentle agitation took place in the water,
as if a heavy shower of rain was falling upon it,
and shortly after a rumbling was heard, resembling the movements of heavy-laden carriages at
a distance on frozen ground. This increased,
and the feet as well as the ear were affected with
a motion something like that felt by a galvanic
battery, or a slight shock from an electric jar.
The leaves of the trees had a tremulous motion,
like that described of the aspen ; the ground
began to tremble, and some buildings at a distance
were toppling down ; but the one in which I
stood was only severely shaken, the wall did not
crack nor give way. The great mass of the
people preferred being in the streets to keeping
in their houses ; they thought that there would be
less danger of being swallowed up in the streets
than of being crushed by the falling of walls in
their houses. There was no screaming, that I
heard ; every one was too much terrified to
scream. Some few were killed by the falling of
houses, even while in the street. The rumbling
noise ceased, and the shocks that followed made
a noise more like the blowing up of a magazine
of powder than of the movements of carriages
on frozen ground. Fire, it is said, was seen to
burst from the earth in several places. The
agony was not entirely gone for nearly two days;
all business was suspended, and men, women, and
children looked at each other as if it were the
last time they were ever to see each other's faces.
Sometimes a tear stood in their eyes, but generally
they were tearless as the marble statue. The
great agitations of life, like its great griefs, are
not relieved by tears. The Chinese are predes-
tinarians, and I was informed that they were

quite unmoved, though still and solemn while nature was in such throes and agonies.

The next day, after all was over, cheerfulness took the place of dismay, and one just arrived could not have known that the people had ever felt a moment's anxiety : so are we constituted. I was alarmed, but not dismayed ; and perhaps, as a stranger, I was in some small degree relieved, from not having any connexions in the city, and from watching the movements of others in such perilous moments. I saw some of the places from which it is said the flames issued at certain periods of the alarm. The governor was constantly in the streets, on horseback, and saw that no confusion took place ; and the priests did not take occasion to alarm the sinner, but soothed him by teaching him to trust in his merciful Creator.

After this, when near the Papua Island, we felt a severe shock of an earthquake. At first I thought we had struck a rock and gone on to it, but I was soon informed that we were not on soundings. Several small blows reached us, and the vessel, for several seconds after, shook and trembled, and kept on her way again. I should rather be at sea in an earthquake than on land, although I have no doubt but vessels have been lost by the phenomenon at sea. Fire pervades earth, air, and sea, and the element is destined to show the Almighty's power in all. Why the action of electricity should not be as wonderful and as uncertain in one element as in another I cannot tell. It seems to be an indispensable agent everywhere, and necessary to the existence of every animal or flower, and to every drop of water that flows on the surface of the earth.

From viewing volcanic remains, one would come to the conclusion that a very considerable part of the land of this globe was once under water. It is said that remains of volcanoes are found in France and Germany, and they certainly are in all parts of South America. How wonderful and sublime is the thought, that those vast masses, the Andes, owe their birth to volcanic power, and that they now burn with ceaseless fires in regions that man is not permitted to reach.

In Manilla I made inquiries of the old inhabitants if they remembered La Perouse; and although forty-three years had elapsed since he was in that port, several gentlemen recollected him, and spoke of him as a most interesting man. He was enterprising and observing ; and the government of France, under the mild and enlightened Louis XVI., selected him as commander of an exploring expedition. The marine of France was then prosperous, but the nation felt that they had not done sufficient in the way of discoveries to put them upon a footing with other modern powers of Europe. Long before he had completed his voyage according to his orders, he had the misfortune to lose one of his captains and several of his scientific corps : still he was not disheartened, but pursued his voyage, and from the frozen regions of the North-west Coast sent home a copy of his Journal, which reached France in safety. This was the last that was heard from him, that is, the last that could be satisfactorily relied upon ; but a thousand vague rumours have been afloat about him. The Journal he sent home was published in a fine style by the government, and shortly afterward it was translated into English, and published in London. This work showed

that he was an acute observer, and that excellent
men went with him.   During the French revolution his fate became a subject of high excitement, and an expedition of discovery, not only of
new islands, but of the fate of La Perouse himself, was fitted out; but nothing was discovered,
at least in this particular.   The excitement was so
great in France at this extraordinary time, and so
much was said in the National Assembly and the
public prints, that all the world began to feel soli-
citous to know what was the end of the intrepid and
intelligent navigator.   In 1825 it was thought that
sufficient information was discovered to satisfy any
one that he was wrecked on the New-Hebrides,
in the Southern Pacific, in south latitude about
11° from the equator, and in eastern longitude
about 170°; but after all, there is no small obscu-
rity about the matter : yet the world were satisfied of two things—first, that La Perouse was
dead, and that this was the most probable story
that had been told of his shipwreck and loss.
With true national enthusiasm, the French spared
no pains to learn any thing that could be discovered of their favourite navigator.   The probable
fate of this brave man has been a subject of
the dramatic muse, and has attracted the attention of youths who had never thought of the
navigator except from the stage.   His wife in
this dramatic scene is supposed to have gone in
search of her husband; but this, I believe, was
sheer fabrication, though it would not be unlike
a Frenchwoman to do so, if she had an opportunity to indulge her inclinations.

   The English government made war with
France while the fate of La Perouse was doubt-
ful; but every cruiser had orders not to interfere

E

with a discovery-ship, but to render them every
assistance in their power. Thus the pursuit of
science has so far softened the nature of man,
that stern war is ordered to lay aside her fierce-
ness, and aid in advancing the knowledge of mankind. This is a noble feature in modern moral
relations, and should never be lost sight of in
future wars. Bonaparte was too busy to make
many efforts at discovery while he had supreme
sway in France, or he was too proud to accept of
British generosity in their preservation. Since
his time France has not done much for discoveries; still they keep a frigate or two out for that
purpose, and the botanical kingdom has been en-
riched by their labours.

The Russians are desirous of being explorers
and discoverers. Kotzebue, the son of the famous
German dramatist, has been employed by Alexander, the autocrat of all the Russias, and his
successor, as a discoverer; and his voyages are
not destitute of interest, though not marked with
many discoveries. His object was rather to watch
the Russian commerce on the North-western
Coast than to give the world any new light upon
science or geography.

After all that is due to Portugal, and Spain, and
France, and Florence, and Venice, England has
done more to give us a knowledge of the size,
shape, and peculiarity of this globe than any
other nation. For more than two centuries her
marine has been the most active and successful.
Her great navigator Sir Francis Drake circum-
navigated the world, and did it in the ordinary
discharge of his duty. He destroyed the armada,
and attacked Spain in her new world with energy
and success; but with what national right the

history of his sovereign must vindicate. The laws of nations were not then very accurately defined. Dampier next followed, but shared little of the glory of a great discoverer. He was among the rovers who harassed the coasts of Chili and Peru. This was, as we should now judge, piracy; but not so then, for both France and England winked at or protected the freebooters of that day. One great object of his adventuring on the Pacific was to find and capture the yearly galleon of Manilla, which was generally very rich; but in this he did not succeed—she escaped his vigilance. He again visited his native country, and was employed in some affairs of maritime enterprise; and changed his character from pilot to captain, always having some enterprise on foot. His voyages are written with great spirit and accuracy: whatever he said of the South Seas has more graphic spirit in it than that of any other voyager I have ever read. His description of a storm, in an open boat, has no equal in print. He was a man of honest principles, notwithstanding he has been called a pirate by Spanish historians.

Some of the Bucaniers were splendid men, although all their actions could not be justified. Circumstances give a direction to the pursuits of men more than principle. The greatest name, however, among discoverers, is that of Captain Cook. He was first sent out as but little more than a sailing-master, and afterward he was sent to Newfoundland as a lieutenant in the navy. His services were acceptable to his employers, for he showed great tact as a commander, and talent as a surveyor of coasts and harbours. In 1768 he was appointed to the command of the Endeavour,

which carried out that scientific scholar, afterward Sir Joseph Banks, and the Swedish naturalist Solander. One great object of this voyage
was to observe the transit of Venus which happened June 3, 1769. They had a fair opportunity to make all the necessary observations at
Otaheite. The neighbouring islands were then
explored, and much new information gained.
The Endeavour then sailed for New-Zealand,
where she arrived in the ensuing autumn. He
spent some time in these seas, according to his
orders, and then returned. Dr. Hawkesworth
assisted Cook in his narrative; and such was the
popularity of the work, that another expedition
was soon fitted out, and the command given to
Cook, who was made a post-captain. Dr. John
R. Forster and his son were sent out as natural-
ists; and some of their observations show that
they were men of science and discernment.
They carried out, also, a painter and an astronomer. This voyage was commenced in July, 1772,
and proceeded as far south as 71°; but was stopped
there by icebergs. The navigator returned in
1775; and in July, 1776, he sailed again. In
this voyage he discovered the Sandwich Islands,
which group he named after Lord Sandwich, then
first lord of the British admiralty. On the 14th
of February, 1779, he was slain in a fracas with
the natives of Owhyee. He was held in high
estimation by all the maritime nations; medals
in honour of his exploits were struck in England,
by order and under the direction of the Royal
Society, and his panegyric was pronounced at
Florence, in all the sweetness of praise that the
Italian language is capable of, and France made
his eulogy a prize question. His voyages have

been perused by every navigator who has since
visited those seas ; and his name is now as familiar to the natives of the Sandwich Islands as
those of their own chiefs.

In this last voyage he was accompanied by an
American gentleman, who has since been as
much distinguished as Cook himself.   John Led-
yard attended Cook as a corporal of marines.   He
had been educated at Dartmouth College, and
came two hundred and thirty miles down the
Connecticut River in a boat made from a pine-
log dug out.   He became afterward a student in
divinity, a schoolmaster, and then a seaman ; and
after a few voyages, having heard that Cook was
going out to the Pacific again, he determined to
accompany him in some capacity or other, if it
was that of a common sailor.   He had, while
quite a young man, made an excursion among the
Indians, and became familiar with their manners
and habits, and conceived a strong passion to explore the world, and make himself acquainted
with all sorts of people.   He was with Cook
when he was killed, and his account differs from
that given by others, but his is undoubtedly the
true one, as he was fearless and had an opportunity to see the rencounter.   On his return to Europe he became acquainted with Franklin and
Sir Joseph Banks, and became a traveller by profession.   He made the attempt to pass through
Northern Asia to the American side of the continent.   This he would undoubtedly have effected
if it had not been for the jealousy of the Russian
government, by whose order he was seized at
Takutz and brought to St. Petersburg.   The
Empress Catherine, being convinced that there
was no politics at the bottom of his mission,

offered him protection, assistance, and employment; but he had had enough of arbitrary governments, and returned to France and England, and was employed by the African Association to explore the interior of Africa. He proceeded on this expedition as far as Cairo, and there died of one of the fevers prevalent in that climate. He was one of those men born for explorers ; curious, patient of labour, above all avarice, and strictly honest in all his exertions, and careful in all his descriptions ; he could be relied on as the best authority for all he said or described. His death was deeply deplored in Europe and America ; for such men are wanted at all times, and more particularly at that time. Since then a spirit of enterprise is awakened, and hundreds are ready to move as soon as a fair opportunity offers.

The present commercial world is indebted as much to American whaling-ships, as to any other source, for information of the Pacific Ocean. They have been indefatigable in noting accurately all their discoveries, and these have been many. The education of these whalers is excellent in mathematics, and they are indisputable in navigation. From the accounts given of whalers from Nantucket, New-Bedford, Stonington, and other places where this trade is carried on, a considerable part of the whole crew are capable of navigating a ship in any seas. A crew of whalers is a singular anomaly in the maritime government—a head, with prerogatives distinctly understood, and a crew who are sharers in all the profits of the voyage. They are not embarrassed with a multiplicity of orders, but have a plain course of duty set before them, and they proceed to discharge it. From these people the secretary of the navy has gained much information. The whaling-ships are numerous ; probably fifty or sixty of them, from different ports, are in the Western and Southern Pacific Ocean the whole of the year. It is not a particular object with them to explore new islands, but they must necessarily find them in their course; and being capable of forming just opinions upon the appearances before them, the sealers have been careful of divulging their discoveries, if there was a chance of future profit from them ; but they have gone farther south than any other navigators, not excepting the explorers themselves.

I often amused the old master mariners by inquiries respecting these matters ; but when I determined to take the voyage, I was also determined to learn as much as I could while absent. The good ladies here know that they are on an island in the Southern Pacific, and that is as much as they care to think about the matter ; and perhaps there may be some in my good city that do not know as yet that the city stands on the Island of Manhattan, and it would be hard, therefore, to censure others for indifference to any thing but the every day occurrences of life. Perhaps, after all, they are the happiest beings whose sphere is confined and whose knowledge is the most limited.

We were now on our voyage homewards. All hearts were light. The distance was every hour diminishing, and the friends we had left in our native land seemed to fill our recollections with delight. We had been absent more than sixteen months, and this time had been so full of incident that it seemed to me longer than all the rest of my life.

It was found, however, soon after our sailing, that our schooner was too deeply laden, and we sailed for Sincapore, to lighten her and put her in proper order for sailing. Notwithstanding my anxiety to get home, I enjoyed this visit to Sincapore, for it is one of the most delightful little places I ever saw. It is but a few years since the English began to build up this city, which bears the same name as the island. This island is situated on the north side of Sincapore Strait; the location is fine for trade, being in a central situation from the China and Java seas, and all the numerous islands in them, and is not far from the coast of China. It will become the mart of traffic from all the Philippine Isles, which are more numerous than the Arabian tales. More than a thousand and one have been discovered and put down in charts or mentioned in the voyages of navigators. The little city was stocked with pearl, tortoise-shell, ambergris, birds of all sorts, and the whole variety that belongs to the great Eastern archipelago. The island has fine water, and a most luxuriant soil, which the enterprising English are putting into fine cultivation. They now raise coffee, sugar-cane, and indigo; in fact, I can hardly mention any thing of a tropical growth that is not to be found there; and there appears, also, a sufficiency of British capital for all the purposes of commerce. Sincapore is one of those places built up at once by the magic of commerce; ten or a dozen years ago, as navigators give it to us from their journals, a few bamboo-huts for the Indian fishermen, or perhaps a miserable Chinese huckster shop, for trading with those who might accidently touch there, was all that was to be seen. Now a regular well-built city is found upon the spot, with wide streets, fine sidewalks, uniform and well-built stone houses, painted entirely white. I see nothing to prevent this city from becoming a splendid one. It is so beautifully situated, that it has the advantage of a sea-air; has no stagnant water; and has a fine back country, to the extent of the island. The forest trees are very large and tall; and on the south side, near the city, is a fine plain, of great extent, so highly cultivated, that it seems one great garden spot. The roads around and through this champaign country are excellent, and on each side of them are rows of trees and shrubs in perpetual verdure. The English merchants understand laying out their grounds much to my taste, and a country-seat here reminds an American that those who speak his language and draw their information from the same sources, have been here. This place is well fortified, and has a considerable garrison in a very healthy situation. The whole population of the island is extensive, but the precise number could not be ascertained; there is probably from fifty to sixty thousand, of Malays, Chinese, Siamese, and all that motley group of different nations that collect near a settlement of Europeans. The English population is about three thousand, and rapidly increasing by enterprising merchant-adventurers, and by the healthy situation for the rearing of children; I think the most so of any Eastern city that could be named. The Chinese here, as in other places in this quarter of the world, are the mechanics, and ingenious ones they are, and work very reasonably. The English merchants here give them better encouragement than they find in Manilla, or any Spanish settlement. The materials for building are abundant and readily procured. The city seems well governed ; every one enjoys his liberty as far as would be of any benefit to him, and he wants no more.

The people under a tropical sun take most of their exercise at the dawn of the morning; a ride or a walk is then most delightful. I never could before understand the full meaning of the convening the senate of the skies at this time of the day :

> " Aurora now, fair daughter of the dawn,
> Sprinkled with rosy light the dewy morn," &c.

but if the reader had ever been at Sincapore, he would have seen the wisdom of the sire of gods in calling his senate together at such a moment. From the earliest dawn the dewdrops are seen trembling on tree, shrub, and flower, and shining all glorious with rosy light. These dewdrops do something more than reflect the rays of light; they distil the sweet essences of all they fall upon, and the sense of smelling is as much regaled as the sight. The odour is not like any thing I ever remember to have enjoyed; it comes not from one aromatic plant, but is the perfume of all " Araby the Blest." As we rode through some of these delightful groves the smell was so ecstatic that it was near overpowering the senses. We met on our way a great number of gentlemen and ladies on horseback, who seemed to have parted with their native silence and gravity, so often remarked upon by the other nations of Europe ; they were as joyous as the morning, and seemed overflowing with happiness. They gave us a most courteous salute, knowing who we were. The English women are truly beautiful.

If they have lost some of their roseate complexion in these tropical suns, which in their native land gives some of them the appearance of almost rude health, they are compensated by fine forms and more interesting looks. They feed more delicately in these climates, eating more vegetables and less solid food than in England. Their being at such a distance from their native land, too, makes them kinder and less aristocratical ; they have a sort of fellow-feeling for strangers, for they recollect how lately it was that they came from home themselves. The ladies of Sincapore are excellent horse-women ; they have a fine breed of English horses, and they ride with great spirit and fearlessness. When the sun rides high in the heavens, these English people return to their houses, and keep quiet until the shades of evening are extended across the pathway ; but the dew begins to fall so soon that the after-part of the day is not so healthy as the morning. How wondrously kind are the laws of nature, that the tree and plant should drink up the poisonous part of the air in the night, and breathe it out a balmy restorative in the morning ! On the 23d of January, about the time the winter has set in in good earnest in my native country, and the face of the earth is covered with snow, and every brook, pond, and river is bound in fetters of ice, we were enjoying a perpetual summer. I often reasoned upon this difference of climate, and asked myself in which region, if I had my choice, I could desire to live ? Here is nothing of anticipation—all is fruition ; but I have my doubts, as we are constituted, if we are so capable of realizing this state as we ought to be. Mortals that are born to be agitated and

tossed about this world require changes of various
kinds; not only those which are brought about
by time, but those of seasons. In our dear
America we have long evenings of social intercourse in the winter; lectures for moral
instruction; sermons for religious improvement;
invigorating sleigh-rides; and mingled with these,
all the hopes of seeing the buddings of spring,
and the enjoyment of summer again; and then
come the fruits of autumn. The sear and decaying leaf falls to the ground, and nature seems
to prepare for repose; and then winter is again
upon us. But in this joyous climate there are
no changes, except that of a shifting of the wind,
or a shock of an earthquake, which is not un-
frequent in all the Eastern regions; though, as far
as I can learn, has never done any injury on this
island. If life is not longer, most certainly health
is better, and more easily preserved in these climates, than in those of perpetual change. The
inhabitants are not liable to those colds which
shock the constitution and bring on consumption
in our climate. Physicians tell us that one-eighth
part of the deaths in our northern climates are
from consumption; I speak more particularly of
females: in this climate no such thing is known.
In all my intercourse with society in Sincapore,
I never saw a dyspeptic or a consumptive female.
If I have hallowed the enjoyments of my native
country, and think the climate of changes is
most preferable, I cannot give up the thought of
the delights of those tropical regions where simple
existence is a bliss; where nature is for ever at
work to rear and to scatter flowers, and never
grows tired of her labours. There is a sort of
revelry of nature which makes in favour of these

climates against ours ; the birds are more joyous,
and the beasts seem to be also ; and surely there is
more life in animated nature than in high northern
latitudes ; and even the horses of European origin are full of spirit and gayety in these bowers
of Eden. The singing of the birds, also, was
delightful here. I had been impressed with the
belief that the gayer the plumage the more dis-
cordant the notes of the feathered tribe ; but this
rule will not hold good. The feather has nothing
to do with the voice. We get such impressions
in America, from the notes of the peacock, the
red-bird, and the woodpecker : but birds of eme-
rald hue and sapphire blaze in these regions of the
sun have notes as sweet as their plumage is
beautiful. I wanted to bring some of these songsters home with me, but was told it could not be
done ; that they could not bear the vicissitudes
of the voyage. The paroquet is often brought to
the United States, but this bird is now no rarity
with us, and is not among the most beautiful of
his native country. My husband and the officers
of the vessel offered to shoot some of all kinds
for me, but as I was no ornithologist, and could
do nothing with classifying them, or in giving
their habits and characters, I could not suffer
them to be shot for me.

On the 23d of January, 1831, a party of us
left the city to visit the highlands of the island,
about six or seven miles west of the town. It
was a pleasant jaunt. After leaving the public
road we found a pathway of ten or twelve feet
wide, cut through a thick forest, and made by
great labour. It is as straight as the nature of
the ground will admit, and the forest trees are so
large and spreading in their branches at the top

that the road is nearly hid from the sun, and seems, a great portion of the way, as if dug through the hill, excepting that the forest admits —thick as it may be—a little more light than could be expected in a subterranean passage. The ride, although we were obliged to go at a snail's pace, is delightful. Birds of ten thousand hues in their plumage are hopping from branch to branch, almost as tame as if in a cage, they are so seldom disturbed. The horses, acquainted with the way, keep a sure footing; and I think there is but little danger unless to one who is desirous of finding dangers where they do not exist. In two hours we gained the summit, but what was its elevation from the sea I was not able to learn, as I doubt whether it has as yet been accurately ascertained, but it certainly must be more than a thousand feet. The view from this elevation is only bounded by the horizon. The forests are of immense size on the sides of this high ground, gradually lessening as you ascend, but still large near the apex. The southern extremity of the Malay peninsula is in sight, and some of the images are distinct with a good glass, without which a voyager never travels a rod from the shore; and by use, one becomes so accustomed to see through this instrument, that the naked eye view would not content the examiner. With the glass we could bring the cascades of the peninsula clearly in sight, which gave a pleasant diversity to the scene. As you descend on the north-west side of the hill, the eye stretches over some highly cultivated plains, that seem one continuous garden for miles; their flowering trees, at this distance, look like shrubbery in full bloom. No scenery is perfect with-

out a water prospect, and this you have here in
great beauty ; you behold the smooth waters of
the strait reflecting the islands that are scattered
around, and which seem to sleep on the surface.
There is a lovely harmony in the prospect; all,
as the painters say, in fine keeping. These
waters are not lifeless neither; the shipping of
numerous nations are seen moving along towards
the harbour of Sincapore, and the little skiff of
the Chinese, built with no taste or shapeliness, is
seen in every direction. Here is every kind of
naval architecture, from the Chinese junk, the
Malay prow, and the Sumatra craft, up to the
fine East Indiaman, uniting size with beauty,
and majesty with a convenient storage. Commerce not only binds nations with a golden chain,
but it gives philosophy food for perpetual reflection. The origin of these nations—their history,
their habits, their pursuits, their dispositions, are
all different; yet they are all the children of the
same great parent, and are all destined to the
same immortality. While philosophizing on all
around, the mind is invigorated by the pure air,
breathed at such an elevation; and we felt as if
belonging to a higher grade of beings than those
pent up in the city. These excursions are common in America: we wander from the Catskill
to the heights of New-Hampshire and Vermont,
as matters of ordinary occurrence ; but seldom
does it happen that such excursions can be made
in these regions. Time will not allow navigators
to take such tours ; or if they could spare a day
or two for such objects, it would, in general, be
unsafe to try it. The natives are so fond of
plunder, and so treacherous as not to be trusted.
In this island, however, all is safe ; where Eng-

lishmen and Americans are, there is no danger of evils from savage men. It is my belief that these two nations are to govern the world, so far as to have their policy and laws adopted in regard to commerce, and liberty extended to all nations, particularly in regard to the abolition of slavery.

On the 24th of January we were ready for sea, and a number of our friends came on board, and took a sail with us for several miles—just far enough to make it pleasant; and then took leave of us with great affection. People so situated are given to hospitality, much more so than those in crowded cities in old and populous countries; they consider every stranger as a visiter, and exert themselves for his happiness. He is to them a sort of link between them and their native land; his presence brings up ten thousand associations that are delightful. We read the same books— are familiar with the same incidents—concur in the same remarks—and have no party interests to distract or confuse us. The first person a female forms an acquaintance with in regions remote from home, is the priest of her own religion, if she happens to find one, or with the physician, if she should happen to need one. Dr. Almadi, of Sincapore, was attentive and kind to us, and has laid us under many obligations of friendship. His two sons are gentlemanly young men, promising merchants in the city. This evening we came to anchor in the Straits of Rio, within a short distance of the shore, and the next morning sailed again through the straits, which we passed early in the evening. This precaution is necessary from the numerous coral reefs scattered along the coast. A navigator cannot be too cautious; hundreds are lost from a want of carefulness. On the 26th, we found ourselves in the Java sea, and thence steered for the Straits of Sunda, and arrived at the eastern entrance thereof on the 28th. We sent a boat ashore; but before she reached there, we perceived with our glasses that the natives were in motion, and so suspiciously so, that a signal was given from the schooner for her to return, which she did without landing. Formerly the natives were not hostile; but it is said that they have latterly got a taste of blood, and have become savage and treacherous. A great deal of information of these seas may be found in Horsburgh's Directory; a work which my husband praised so highly that I studied it as a country justice does the Farmer's Almanac, not only for dates, but for matters of opinion. This cool and intrepid navigator spent a good proportion of his life in the East India seas, for the East India Company, and was a great matter-of-fact man, to which were united sound judgment and wonderful perseverance. Such a man is truly a benefactor to mankind; he shows us how to shun evil, and how to take the best advantage of our situation. This East India Company, whatever politicians may say about monopoly and exclusive privileges, has done more to make safe the navigation of those seas, than all the world besides. Governments are not generally disposed to do much for a general interest; our own has hardly made a chart for the navigator. I was mortified that in every country we visited, we had to sail by charts of other nations; we even left our own "sublime port," the harbour of New-York, by an English chart. I am not wise enough to understand this,

when next to the English we are the greatest
wanderers over the globe, and have as much at
stake as any other nation but the English everywhere, from the north to the south pole. Nor
had we any books on board written by our
countrymen, giving us particulars of those seas
which we visited. I have understood, however,
that one or two volumes have lately been written
upon this subject by our countrymen, which give
some account of a part of our course, but I have
not seen them ; we had nothing of the kind with
us when we sailed. Our books were generally
English, and to these alone we had recourse.
Much may be written, however, without inter-
fering with what has been done.

These seas are dangerous. At our tops were
stationed men with arms to prevent being boarded.
The Malays are proverbially treacherous, but
when met with spirit are not persevering in their
hostilities. They are proud, revengeful, and ava-
ricious. Their climate makes them indolent, and
of course they know but little of the blessings of
industry. They have something of the taste of
the Chinese in their manufactures, but are too
lazy to improve. Their dress is singular to us,
but all the Asiatics resemble each other in dress,
that is, all the civilized nations. They are Mohammedans in their religion, and wear turbans on
their heads, differing but little from those of the
Turks ; but they are more tenacious of all religious observances than even the Turks. They
deal in mysteries and study magic, pretending to
great proficiency in the art. Although the Christian religion has not entirely freed the world from
this superstition, yet it has done much towards
driving it from Christendom. Their professed

magicians now, for aught I know, are held in as
high veneration by the common classes of people
as those of the olden time were at the courts
of Babylon. It is a great mistake with us to
suppose that these Malays are ignorant of letters ; I have seen some fine pieces of chirography
from them. Most of them carry charms and
amulets about them, as preservatives against sor-
ceries. Like all the Eastern nations, they make
ablutions a part of their religious ceremonies. It
is said that the Koran prescribes all these ceremonies, and it does,—but Mahomet found such customs prevalent among the people, and, with great
sagacity, made them a part of his religious creed.
The laws among the Malays are such as generally
prevail with the eastern nations, only they come
in a more barbarous form than those found in
some others. They are revengeful, and often
take the law into their own hands when insulted.

We were once more in the Indian Ocean, on
our way towards the shores of America. The
trade-winds are a great curiosity to one who
pretends not to read nature deeply ; you find
them blowing steadily for six months one way,
and then change and blow six months the other :
but wo betide those who are caught in those seas
at the time they are shifting. At that season, the
winds are variable, and storms of rain and thunder gather up and make the navigation difficult
and dangerous. In crossing these seas, the
voyager, like myself, who had nothing to do but
read for amusement, can find various theories respecting the causes of all these remarkable things ;
yet, perhaps, it is the best way often to time one's
voyage in such a manner as not to be in danger of
meeting these perilous seasons. We experienced

near Java Head variable winds and heavy thunder and lightning, until we took the south-east trades, which was about the 12th of February, 1831. We continued our passage to the south and west until we passed in sight of the Isle of France and the island of Madagascar.

As we came near the Isle of France, I most earnestly wished my husband to touch at it, for here I understood reposed the remains of Mrs. Harriet Newell, a missionary from New-England. Her life was an interesting one, and the latter part of it full of incident. She was a daughter of Mr. Moses Atwood, a merchant of Haverhill, a beautiful town on the banks of the Merrimack. Her family was highly respectable, and she received a good education. About the year 1806 or 1807, she became religious, and was active in her piety. Her correspondents were numerous, and she wrote like one deeply imbued with divine grace. In the midst of her zeal she was a pattern of modesty and moderation; she was kind to all about her, and while taking a lead in matters of religion, she was strictly attentive to every domestic duty. Her name became familiar in all the churches, and when the board of missions for India in the United States had selected several promising young gentlemen, for the purpose of sending them into the East to spread the glad tidings of the gospel, Mr. Newell was one of them, and Divine Providence brought him acquainted with Miss Atwood.

Missionary labours and fatigues and dangers were the constant subject of conversation, of preaching, and prayer. She was from the first attentive, and at length her mind was wholly engaged in the great cause. She set about with

her friends preparing some articles which it was
thought might be wanted, for those about to take
upon themselves the arduous and perilous undertaking. She often spoke to Mr. Newell with so
much fervour and affection for the cause, that he
ventured to ask her hand, and to request her to
share in the great work of saving souls with him.
She had not contemplated the subject before, but
after taking the advice of her religious friends,
and of her family, and seeking direction from
Heaven,—although there were many doubts and
some opposition,—she made up her mind, and
engaged in the cause with her whole soul. It was
enough to shake the firmest mind, to think of
leaving home—sweet home,—of parting with
mother, sisters, and brothers, and a train of dear
friends, made dearer by religious bonds of affection ; but she surmounted all, put her trust in the
Lord, and took her departure for the Indies, as an
humble missionary in the cause for which her
Saviour died.

   " I never shall forget," says one of her male
friends, " the hour of Mrs. Newell's departure.
The circle were engaged in prayer, and a clergyman with a harsh voice and strong lungs was
leading in the devotions ; he struck with no gentle
hand the chords of the heart, and the little group
could not refrain from tears and sighs : all were
convulsed at the thought that they might never
see her face again. When the clergyman had
ended, she cast her eyes around, and fearful of the
effect of this impression, in a voice sweet as an
angel's, she began to speak to her distressed
friends. She represented to them that her beloved Saviour was everywhere a protector of those
who obeyed his precepts ; that he could soften

the rage of intolerable suns, and break the iron heart of obdurate man ; that he could make the dying bed as soft as the downy pillow ; and that as life was short, and the time for doing good limited, it was for each one to go his way and commence his labours. She spoke of the union of souls by the influence of prayer ; she said that there was no such thing as distance between the good and their Father in heaven; that humble means in the history of man had brought about great ends; and that even she, an humble sinner, might be the means of saving a soul, which would be sufficient reward for all she might suffer. She commended all to God, the staff and stay of the widow, the father of the orphan, and the consolation of all who sought him. Never had mortal words a kinder effect. The sobs ceased, the trembling voices of her friends assumed a firmer tone, and their farewells had no convulsions in them. As she turned to depart, her eye caught that of the narrator of this scene ; they had once been intimate friends, but he, as a man of the world, had smiled at what he called the enthusiasm of the revival, and had seldom seen her after she left the gay circle of her youth ; she stepped forward without any embarrassment, stretched out her hand, which was grasped with no little emotion, and with an affectionate smile said, ' My dear L., the time will come when you will think better of all this ; my prayers shall be for your conversion. Have no fears for me ; I go on my Saviour's errand ; may we meet in heaven.' She gave them a benediction, and he could not but see and feel, that

> ' While on their knees they lingered yet,
> There fell a light more lovely far
> Than ever came from sun or star.' "

Mrs. Newell went to India, and suffered much from the fatigues of missionary travels, finding more difficulties in the way than was anticipated. Her constitution was never strong, and fell under her sufferings ; she expired at the Isle of France, on the 30th day of November, in the 19th year of her age. She lived long enough to show the sincerity of her religious zeal, and her willingness to die in such a cause. She wrote some letters to her friends, breathing the airs of holiness, which have reached the hearts of many who were fainting and despairing on the way to Zion, and given them strength to bear the heat and burden of the day. If she could have found a resting-place, she would have laboured assiduously in the great work she went out to perform ; but as it was, she only showed the spirit that was within her. I understood that an American ship-master, a man of piety, found her grave without stone or name in this island, and reared the best one he could for the time. In some future day, the traveller from the land of her fathers will build the proud mausoleum over her remains.

I had heard before my departure from the United States, that her friend and fellow-labourer, who had long been in the vineyard of the Lord, Mrs. Judson, had departed this life also. She was a woman of still finer talents than Mrs. Newell, and lived to do much good. She was, as fame relates the story, an ambassadress of the King of Ava to the British, when war and desolation were carried into his territories ; and by her means the effusion of human blood was stopped. The world may, and do, censure the practice of sending out females with the missionaries ; but I am convinced that men will do but little good without their

wives and families. The ignorant natives feel
the influence of example more than of precept,
and when they see whole families living in peace
and domestic affection, they strive to imitate
them ; they go to the hut where the missionary
and his family reside, and seeing the neatness
and all the little conveniences which exist there,
they feel a desire for the same things arising in
their own minds ; and will labour, although indolent by habit, to acquire such comforts as can
easily be attained in these fruitful countries of the
East. The women first show a love of dress, then
of cleanliness of person, and every step in the progress of imitation is so much gained in the march
of civilization.

It was delightful to see at New-Zealand how
much this imitative spirit had effected, even in the
manner of taking their food and receiving their
guests. The queen was quite a lady, while the
king, as I have before mentioned, was making
himself an English orator. There is another
reason why men should take their families with
them on a mission ; they are more contented, and
are more steadily engaged in the great work than
they would be alone. The native females are
taught sewing and household affairs, and impressed with the necessity of going on with the
great work of mental improvement and religious
advancement. In the diffusion of even our holy
religion, in the days of our Saviour's appearance,
the women were among the first and most faithful of his disciples ; they listened to his doctrines,
sought him through life, and followed him to the
tomb. Those who take up the cross must expect
deprivations and long-suffering ; they must leave
father and mother, and all the world, for the good
of their fellow-men. If ever there was sincerity

anywhere, it is in an honest missionary's heart.
They will be treated as fools and madmen by
some; and, cut off from all the charms of cultivated society, they will go down to the grave
generally unhonoured and unknown, but their reward will be an incorruptible crown.

In this sea the phenomenon of the luminous
appearance of the surface of the water was more
remarkable than I had ever witnessed it at any
other place. At night the sea appears one blaze
of light. I have watched this extraordinary appearance many evenings as a subject of curiosity
and pleasure, and was anxious to know what light
philosophy had thrown on the matter. I looked
at all the books we had, in hopes of finding the
causes of it, but after a while formed my own
opinion upon the subject, although I do not pre-
tend to give it as one of certainty where others
have been in doubt. Father Bourzes, a Jesuit,
in 1704, marked this phenomenon in his voyage
to India. This class of men, who have been
a subject of censure for so many years, have been
the precursors of most of our knowledge of the
appearances of nature, as well as of the moral
condition of man. Among their faults was not
that of apathy or ignorance. The finest descriptions the world now has of all the wonders of
nature came from these holy missionaries; the
description of sea-objects, the soil, climate, cataracts, and prairies, came from them; they encom-
passed sea and land to make proselytes, and kept
eyes and ears open in every step of their progress.
Of their religion I have nothing to say; it is
not my religion. The pious father notes the
singular appearance of the sea, but does not venture to give any reason for its causes. He was

F

going to a new world to guide the heathen in the paths of religion ; but he was also, according to the instructions of his order, obliged to notice every thing remarkable in his tour. This phenomenon was discussed by the philosophers of Europe with considerable acumen ; but nothing satisfactory was given until of late years. The first solution was that of electricity, and for a while this was satisfactory to most navigators; but on the voyages of Captain Cook, in 1772, '3, '4, and '5, Mr. Forster started a new theory, which had so much plausibility in it, that it was not questioned for many years. This was, that the singular appearance was caused by animalculæ, which, analogous to the firefly, had the power, at pleasure, of emitting light, and did so whenever the surface of the ocean was slightly agitated. This many experiments seemed to prove, and the doctrine became general, for there were many facts going to show that his opinion was correct; and it is now conceived that there are many sea-worms or insects that emit light in the ocean. But the best opinion now extant is that of Mr. Couton's, that this appearance arises from putrefactions in the sea. The phosphoric appearance of a fish in a short time after he was caught led him to make many experiments, which go far to show that his solution was just. He put fish into a quantity of salt water, and marked the effects of their putrescence on the appearance of the water ; and ascertained that in proportion to the decay of the fish was the luminous appearance of the water. These particles of decayed fish, being lighter than the water, rise to the surface, and on a gentle agitation emit the phosphoric light which makes so wonderful an illumination. This appearance

is more observable near land than at a great distance from it; and it is well known that the great
mass of the inhabitants of the deep are near the
continents and islands. Perhaps in no situation
of all the vast expanse of the ocean is this phenomenon more distinct than around the islands
of the Southern Pacific. The wonders of the
land man has been examining from the birth of
creation; but of the treasures and population of
the ocean he has, as it were, just commenced his
observations. The innumerable productions of
the ocean are astounding; not only may it be said

> " Full many a gem of purest ray serene
> The dark, unfathomed caves of ocean bear,"

but not a tithe of its population is as yet known.
The earth, using this term for the land only, with
all its nations of men, its beasts and birds, its
creeping things—countless millions in all,—has a
sparse population compared with the sea. If the
death of these, by violence and natural decay, do
not " incarnadine the sea," it is very natural that
the remains of these innumerable hosts—for death
happeneth to all things belonging to our globe—
probably rise to the surface, and float on in rays
of light; and why not another emblem that the
ashes of our frames sown in corruption will rise
to light and glory in another form ? It surpasses
the wonderful,—it is indeed miraculous, that so
many things should exist in the waters under the
earth. Who can look at the leviathan of the
ocean, spouting and blowing, and playing in the
mighty deep, a terror to man when he first saw
him in the tremendous majesty of his bulk and
strength, now subservient to man, as a thing of

no power compared with human sagacity, and
the very essence of the monster reduced to the
purpose of illuming his halls, or of chasing away
the shades of night from the nursery of his babes,
and doubt that man had power given him over
all that live upon the land or in the sea? The
luxurious Romans knew nothing of the brilliancy
of a sperm candle.

The fisheries, in all parts of the world, furnish
no small part of the food of man, and yet there is
no diminution of the stock. The great fish, if
Dr. Mitchill will allow me to call a whale a fish,
are no doubt diminished; but it is not in the
power of man to destroy the race of them, which
according to the best accounts of ichthyologists,
produce as ten thousand, and even to a million
for one taken yearly. Millions of the cod are caught
on the northern shores of America yearly, yet no
diminution has ever been perceptible.

The analogy between things in the water and
on the land has often been a subject of inquiry
and discussion, and perhaps there is in it something of reality. There are sea-dogs, sea-elephants, and sea-horses; but in many respects the
resemblance is fanciful: but to man, the constituted lord of all, I do not believe that the sea
furnishes the slightest resemblance. We women
have been complimented by sister mermaids; but
I believe all this race have been females, even in
fable. The wonders of the great deep, I believe,
will never be fully discovered; but there is no
necessity for indulging in creations of fancy when
there is enough of fact to satisfy any one.

When I playfully adverted to the opinions of
Dr. Mitchill respecting the whale, I intended no
disrespect to the memory of that learned man.

He was indeed a learned man, familiar and kind as learned. He had the happiest faculty of making himself understood, and his descriptions, in his lectures and publications, are all simple, accurate, and beautiful. He was a great lover of nature, and studied her laws profoundly. He discussed every thing, from the huge whale and ponderous mastodon, to the microscopic shell and the animated dust of a fig-leaf. He seemed inspired by every muse in the department of each. His own collection of natural curiosities was a rare one ; at once an evidence of his knowledge, his industry, and his taste. He made himself master of so many facts that he was a living chronicle of the history of nature, as well as of the deeds of men. He was acquainted with the nomenclature of every science, and had every term ready at his tongue's end ; but he never darkened his subject by a display of them, for he explained the etymology of the term he used, and the necessity there was of the word to convey an accurate meaning. The great doctor believed much, because he knew much ; and with all his knowledge, he was as communicative as those who were bursting with their first rays of intelligence. The doctor was extensively known at home and abroad ; he held a correspondence with some of the most learned men of the age, and every one thought him truly a great man. Future times will hold him higher than the present does ; when his favourite pursuits become more fashionable than they now are. I understand that great exertions are making by intelligent members of this community in the city of New-York, and other parts of the country, to increase the number and respectability of Lyceums.

On the 4th of March we spoke an East Indiaman, from Canton, on her voyage to London.
Captain Gates, the commander, most kindly
offered us any assistance we might stand in need
of, but our provisions were abundant, and we
could only acknowledge our obligations for his
kind offers.   There is a courtesy growing out of
circumstances which becomes a habit, and from
that passes to a principle. Those who have been in
want know how to lend their assistance to others,
and every mariner, with all the foresight and
prudence in the world, must, at times, be in want
of the necessaries of life.   The offers of Capt.
Gates were so kind, that I was almost sorry to
find that owing to our superior sailing he was
nearly out of sight in a few hours.   How much
happier would our lives pass on shore, if we were
employed in offering kindnesses to one another,
and in watching to see what good we could do our
fellow-travellers through the world.   Selfishness
seems to belong to great cities.   It is not found
where the inhabitants are few ; or at least it is not
so perceptible.

CHAPTER VI.

Saldanha Bay—Refitted—Visit to the Cape—Description of Saldanha Bay—Table Mountain—Comparison between the Animals found at the Cape and the Race of Men—Description of the Condor—His Habits and Character—The Albatross—His Habits and Character—Superstitions in Regard to the Condor—Hottentots and Lions—Character of the Lion—The Elephant—Ostriches; Description of, and their Character—Accuracy of the Scripture Account—Garrison at the Cape—Camoens and his Lusiad—The Character of this commercial Epic—Fate of the Author—Reflections upon the Restrictions upon Trade.

On Thursday, the 10th of March, we came in sight of the Cape of Good Hope, but it was some miles distant, whence we steered for Saldanha Bay, and came to anchor there on the 12th. All hands were as busy as the inhabitants of the city of New-York are on the first day of May. They were taking down sails, splicing ropes, mending, patching, darning, and cleaning; for a few days, all were as much engaged as carmen, chamber-maids, and housewives at the stirring time I have mentioned. It is not wonderful that our schooner should be out of repair in her sails and rigging, when it is recollected that she had been from home more than sixteen months.

On the 14th I accompanied my husband on shore, and we received a most cordial welcome. He had been here before and made several acquaintances, who were now emulous to show every kindness to his wife.

The Bay of Saldanha is the place where the

fleet anchored to protect the English troops under
Sir David Barard, to land for the last conquest
of the Cape. This was a fine place to anchor,
and the garrison of the Cape was at too great a
distance to give them any trouble while landing.
We visited the village, and found the people quite
contented under the British government. Sir
David had seven thousand troops under his command ; and although he was met with great
courage by the Dutch commander and the forces
under him, yet the action was soon decided, and
the British have had the possession of the Cape
ever since. It is a fine stopping-place for ships
on their way to India, and sufficient of all necessaries can be furnished at short notice. The
English thought this place of much consequence
to them ; and although they had taken the place
once before and given it up by treaty, at this
second conquest they thought it better to retain it.

The Cape of Good Hope is situated in latitude
33° 55′ south, and longitude 18° 24′ east. It was
discovered by the Portuguese in 1493, and was
called by the discoverer, Bartholomew Diaz,
Cabo dos Tormendos—the Stormy Cape,—for he
experienced much bad weather there ; but his
more sagacious monarch, John II. King of Portugal, named it the Cape of Good Hope, as he
entertained the hope of finding the way to
India by doubling this cape, which was soon
after done by Vasco de Gama. The Portuguese
never formed any settlement at the Cape ; they
had but few people to spare for colonizing any
but the fairest portions of their discoveries. The
Dutch, about 1650, took possession of it, and
drove away the Hottentots. They wanted it for
a watering-place, and found no difficulty in re-

ducing the ignorant and miserable race of savages who were natives of the country to slavery. These Hottentots are small in size, but are much esteemed as slaves, for they are the most abject of all the slaves in the world. The Malays and other slaves, when goaded by illtreatment, have some flashes of resentment about them; but these abject wretches have none. The south and west of the Cape are washed by the ocean, and on the north a long range of mountains is seen, some of which reach the point of perpetual congelation. The population of the whole country now owned by the English is very sparse, not giving one inhabitant to a square mile. It contains a great variety of soil, but the drought is excessive at certain seasons, and there is no vegetation for many months in the year. When we were there, we saw large tracts of country blooming with a great variety of flowers, and affording abundance of herbage, which shortly before this was as dry and steril as a clay heap.

The Table Mountain is one vast mass of rock, rising in naked majesty three thousand five hundred and ninety-six feet in height! Its very look is frightful. Some persons, it is said, have reached its summit, but it seemed to me to be accessible to none but the great birds of heaven. The condor and the eagle are seen in the gray of the morning poising around its summit, as if in scorn of the powers of man. It is thought that they frequently rise with their prey to the sides and top of this mountain, to devour it in peace. After gazing a few minutes through a good glass the mass seems too heavy for the earth, and you feel as though it must sink, and carry with it all around you. The rock is of primitive formation;

F 3

it has been there ever since the birth of creation, and probably will stand there until

> " Wrapt in fire the realms of ether,
> And heaven's last onset shakes the world below !"

This rock was not smote by the hand of the prophet, for no water gushes from it except what drizzles down from snows or dews. If this sublime mass had been near tasteful Greece or poetic Italy, how much it would have assisted the writers of the works of imagination ! There, not a mountain rears its head unsung, nor a brook that babbles along, but has been celebrated in all the charms of verse. Camoens alone has made this region a subject for the muse.

It is worthy of remark, that while the beasts and birds of this region are wonderful in size and strength, the race of men should be so inferior in their proportions. Until our times, the eagle was considered by ornithologists as the bird of Jove, holding supreme sway over all the feathered race. He was described as soaring higher, and keeping longer on the wing, than all others of the air. For majesty, strength, and vision, he had no compeer, but modern discoveries have robbed him of all his superiority in these regions, as well as among the Andes. The condor is now enthroned in his place. Until this age, the condor was ranked among the creatures of fable, with the roc, of Arabian imagination and description, or with the wonders of Gulliver, in his travels. Swift undoubtedly made his stories of gigantic and diminutive nature as a satire upon the tales of travellers, but in our time his sarcasm has lost something of its effect from deeper investigation

MRS. MORRELL'S NARRATIVE. 131

and more patient researches. The condor of Africa is at the head of the vulture tribe. His size is twice that of the American eagle; some of them indeed have been killed, whose extended wings measured twelve or fourteen feet. He is almost constantly on the wing, and soars at a sightless distance above the earth. This upper region is truly his abode—the scene of all his joys; and he comes down to the ground only to secure his food. He has the scent of the common vulture, and the eye of the eagle, enlarged even in greater proportion than his body compared with that of the eagle. His claws and beak are in proportion to the spread of his wing. He is coarse and vulgar in his food; and, notwithstanding all that has been said by the poets of ancient and modern times, so is the eagle. The Hebrew description of the productions of nature, after all, is generally the most accurate. The Bible says that where the carcass is, there are the eagles gathered together. The condor, driven by hunger, scents or sees from his sublime height what is lying or moving on the earth, and comes to seize it with almost incredible velocity. He feeds on dead carcasses when they can be found, but otherwise it attacks the flocks and the herds. He has been known to associate with others to attack full-grown bullocks, and to destroy them; but from his very nature he is generally a solitary bird. The Table Mountain is hardly sufficiently elevated for him to relish his prey, which he often ascends with; he requires a keen air. The condor has been caught at the Cape, and in South America, and brought to the United States, where he has been examined thoroughly. He is in every respect a wonder, and amazing stories are said to be current among the Hottentots of the prodigious

size and strength of this bird, such as their having been seen with an elephant in their claws.
These stories go to show that even the most stu-
pid of human beings have some imagination:
Asia does not originate all the wondrous things
in story. The condor flies like the eagle, except
that he is slower in his first movements, from the
great extent of his wings. His feathers are closer
and smoother than the eagle's, and he can rest in
the loftiest regions of the air for a long time without any apparent motion, but probably, like the
eagle, he has the power of moving the lesser
feathers while the wings seem perfectly still.

Turning from a look at the mountains, and
extending your gaze over the ocean, a sea-bird
of equal size and larger wing may every day be
seen. The albatross is remarkable in his habits
as well as in size. He is a web-footed bird, resembling in some degree the domestic goose as
to the shape of its head and body; but the bill is
more hooked than that of the goose. The great
length of wing gives the albatross superior swift-
ness in flight to all other sea-birds; and, large as
he is, he skims with the fleetness of a swallow
over the water, catching every thing that comes
in his way. He is a great feeder, and sometimes
acts the glutton to such an extent as to be easily
taken while resting on the smooth surface of the
sea. It is amusing to watch his flight after the
flying-fish, he poises, scales, and turns so adroitly.
The albatross appears to have no regular home,
but courses over half a world for his food at
different seasons of the year; he is not only
found at the Cape of Good Hope and on the
North-west Coast, but also at times in the Aus-
tral seas. He flies so easily that he clears him-

self of a storm by rising above it, and keeping himself there until the whirlwind has passed away. The albatross is tame, but not courageous, for he is often beaten to death by smaller birds, and makes but a feeble resistance. The extent of their wings, when spread, is ten or twelve feet in general, but they grow to a much larger size. They are never taken for food, even by the Indians; they are too coarse and oily for food for any thing. The albatross is seldom killed by American or European sailors; they have some superstition that it betides ill-luck to kill them. Perhaps this may arise from the fact that this bird has often visited vessels farther from land than any others, and, as the sailors say, has taken more pains to board them than all the rest of the feathered tribe. Some of the largest of these birds have been killed and brought to this country, but in general their lives are spared, for it requires a very brave man to oppose a superstition entertained among mariners, as all the misfortunes of the voyage are always charged upon any violence done to a settled prejudice. Ignorant men will more readily do violence to a positive command of their Maker than to a fixed error of the imagination. Coleridge, the poet, has made much use of this superstition in his poem called the

RIME OF THE ANCIENT MARINER.

"The ice was here, the ice was there,
  The ice was all around:
  It cracked and growled, and roared and howled,
  Like noises in a swound!

At length did cross an albatross;
  Through the fog it came;
  As if it had been a Christian soul,
  We hailed it in God's name.

It ate the food it ne'er had eat,
And round and round it flew ;
The ice did split with a thunder-fit,
The helmsman steered us through !

And a good south wind sprang up behind ;
The albatross did follow,
And every day, for food or play,
Came to the mariner's hallo !

In mist or cloud, on mast or shroud,
It perched for vespers nine ;
Whilest all the night, through fog smock white,
Glimmered the white moonshine.

God save thee, ancient mariner,
From the fiends that plague thee thus !
Why look'st thou so ?' With my crossbow
I shot the albatross !

The sun now rose upon the sight ;
Out of the sea came he,
Still hid in mists, and on the left
Went down into the sea.

And the good south wind still blew behind,
But no sweet bird did follow,
Nor any day, for food or play,
Came to the mariner's hallo !

And I have done one hellish thing,
And it would work 'em wo ;
For all averred I had killed the bird
That made the breeze to blow ;
'Ah, wretch !' said they, 'the bird to slay
That made the breeze to blow !' "

The earth here, as well as the air, teems with
wonders. The lion of the Cape is the largest and
fiercest in the world, and although he has been
driven from many places where he once roamed,
he still holds his ground in Southern Africa.
His roar is often heard in the abodes of Europeans ; but he does not often make his appearance
near the habitations of men. The Hottentots
have no fears of the lion, nor of any wild animal ;

they contend that all that are ferocious in the
forests or deserts are afraid of man, and this is
probably the case.   A lion never attacks a man
unless he is famished for food ; and then his
hunger is generally superior to his courage.
They prey on the harmless antelopes, and never
venture to attack the elephant.   Many an officer
in these regions has, with the help of natives and
dogs, gained laurels for bravery in lion hunting
who did not risk much in the contest.

The lion, like all other creatures of greatness,
has been extolled and abused ever since he has
been known.   The Arabians, it is said, have about
fifty names for this monarch of the plains.   His
strength is not at all overrated by any, but his
magnanimity has often been questioned.   Notwithstanding all the stories of ancient times, of
Androcles and the lion, and of the many other
legends of those ages, modern writers on natural
history have made the lion a cowardly, sneaking,
miserable cat, with only more strength than his
enemies, and without half the courage of a terrier
dog.   The truth is between these historians.
His magnanimity may sometimes be mistaken
for cowardice, and his prudence for fear.   That
the lion has strong affections no one who knows
his history can for a moment doubt ; and we
have all seen enough of him in a state of slavery
to know that he has some generous traits in his
character.   It is from a well-authenticated account of a lion and a friendly dog that I extract
the following. — In a caravan which was ex-
hibited a few years since in the United States, a
large lion was the head of the show, and a monstrous sized dog was his master's faithful friend.
On some occasion the whole caravan grew restiff.

and the keeper, somewhat alarmed, requested the
audience to retire, inviting them to return on the
morrow. The lion growled, and snapped his
teeth at his keeper; the dog saw it, and in a fit
of indignation bit the lip of the lion. This
brought the latter animal to his senses, and he
crouched and groaned and moaned, and refused
that night and the next day to taste a morsel of
food, but kept up a look of contrition towards the
dog. The owner was apprehensive of losing his
property, and entreated the dog to make up with
the lion. At length he succeeded in getting the
dog to approach the lion's cage and lick his
wound. The lion's joy was excessive; he
growled his affection, and seemed quite frantic
in his demonstrations of happiness.

The ponderous elephant never goes out of his
way to attack a man; he also is afraid of him.
Whole droves of elephants will pass within a few
rods of a hunter without giving him the least
fear. The almost naked African traverses the
deserts or the forests as fearlessly as if he had
dominion given him over the fowls of the air
and the beasts of the field as distinctly as it was
given to Adam in the days of primeval innocence.
From the enormous tusks which are brought to
this market from the country, the size of the
giant of the forest may in some measure be calculated. Some of these tusks weigh over a hundred
pounds.

These are not all the wonders of the woods
and the sands. Ostriches are plentiful here;
many are brought every year for sale to the Cape
by the natives. A full-grown ostrich is from
eight to eleven feet in height, and the most
awkward looking bird that ever was seen; but

some portion of its feathers are delicate and beautiful. They were used as an ornament for a female headdress probably long before the records of man began, as they were when Vasco de Gama discovered the Cape, and would now be if the natives were not slaves; or if those who were not bondmen and bondwomen had not found that these plumes could be exchanged for something which they preferred to ostrich feathers. The ostrich is often hunted, but such is the fruitfulness and the abundance of food for the bird, that they are still found in great numbers; and their eggs are served up at every great feast given among the officers of the garrison as a delicacy.

Modern writers have stated that the ostrich incubates her eggs, and has as great a regard for them as any other bird; now this assertion appears to me unfounded. The ostrich cannot set upon her eggs; there is no joint in her legs, that will allow her to bring her body upon her nest. Job is worth a hundred philosophers upon the subject: " *Gavest thou the goodly wings unto the peacock, or wings and feathers unto the ostrich?*" " *which leaveth her eggs in the earth, and warmeth them in the dust; and forgetteth that the foot may crush them, or that the wild beast may break them. She is hardened against her young ones, as though they were not hers.*

An observing philosopher, who had spent the better part of his life in Asia, an officer, once gave this solution of the subject: The ostrich starts from the forest to the desert to deposite her eggs. She lays two eggs, which are deeply covered with the sand; then seven or eight more, which are but partially covered. The first produce

young ones, who, as soon as they have broken
the shell, begin to feed upon the roasted eggs
which have been deposited there for food, until
they get strong enough to set out on their journey to the wilderness. This is full of wisdom,
and resembles all the accounts which have been
given of the ostrich.

It is now a matter of fact to all the hunters of
the ostrich, that at *"what time she lifteth up
herself on high she scorneth the horse and his
rider."* In catching her now, one fresh horse
succeeds another until the ostrich is tired down.
It is a most extraordinary fact, that the stomach
of this bird, made, as it is said, to consume fruits
alone, should have such powers of digestion as
to consume lead, iron, or almost any other metal.
Those brought to the United States are generally
destroyed by trying this experiment too often.
This tall bird is good-natured, and the ancients
thought marked with folly; but modern times have
learned to discriminate awkwardness from folly,
and adroitness from wisdom. It is said that when
the ostrich hides his head among the weeds, he
thinks he is not seen; does not even wise man
do pretty much the same?

The garrison here is large, and is composed,
generally, of well educated men. The society is
much better than it was under the Dutch government. The staid and solemn character of the
Dutch may make a place a good permanent
residence, but they do not give society any of the
musical spirit which makes it delightful on a
short visit. They catch not the graces of the
passing hour; I speak of those who have lately
come from their native land. The descendants
of the Dutch in my native state are not only

among the most solid portion of the community, but also make up a highly respectable part of fashionable as well as of valuable society.

The Cape of Good Hope promises, under present auspices, to be an opening for civilization to enter Africa ; and not half of the wonders and the treasures of this country are as yet known.

The region over which we have lately traversed, and where we now were, was one of epic grandeur, although still so much unknown. Camoens, who was born soon after Gama doubled the stormy Cape, and who wrote before Shakspeare or Milton, made the voyage of Vasco de Gama the subject of an heroic poem. Among the first recollections of this poet were the tales of the adventures of this great navigator. Delighted with his romantic theme, Camoens, who had tried his hand in madrigals and sonnets, in early life, contemplated an epic, which he called the Lusiad ; and to bring it to perfection he visited those seas and countries which had been discovered by Gama. His life was one of trials and misfortunes ; he lived with kings and expired with beggars. He held honourable employment under some of the viceroys, and at one time accumulated no small portion of wealth, which was afterward lost in a shipwreck. He was too open, bold, and satirical to live in a court of parasites and flatterers, and he despised the whole of them, from the highest to the lowest. He died with the patriotic expression " *Oh my country !* " on his lips, and with more reason than most men who have used this lamentation. Portugal was then the first of all the maritime powers, but Spain and other countries were in the days of Camoens contending with, and indeed rivalling Portugal. The epic of Camoens is divided into ten books, and, for the age, was full of poetry. To his credit, too, after all the fiction he has introduced, sometimes revelling in heathen mythology, mingled with scriptural allusions, it abounds in truths. He carries his hero around the Cape, and brings him in competition with all the Moorish princes, who had held the best portions of the traffic of the Indies for ages. His struggles with these warlike merchants are finely described, and all the new sensations which this mighty struggle produced. Everywhere, after his time, the navigators of these regions inscribed on the bark of trees wherever they landed this proud inscription, "TALENT DE BIEN FAIRE." The reader of the Lusiad of Camoens will find in it at all times many beautiful passages; but when reading it on the very spots he describes, it seems to bring author and reader together, although nearly three centuries have elapsed since the poet visited them. Camoens was surely an observer of nature, as well as an accurate historian. He describes the highborn cavalier preparing for his departure to unknown regions with graphic accuracy and in an elegant style. De Gama leads all his sailors to a chapel the night before he departs, and spends the night in prayer. On the road from this place to his fleet his friends met him, and prayers, tears, and wailings filled the air. Full of his glory he moved firmly onward: no one but those who have parted with friends to go on long and perilous voyages can realize this part of the scene. Oh! it is true to nature; it is true to the life, humbler life than the proud Spanish don. Many a mother, wife, and sister, at such times, has breathed in spirit the lines of Camoens:

"Curs'd be the man who first on floating wood
Forsook the beach, and braved the treacherous flood !"

But this feeling is soon lost in a nobler one, which incorporates the pride of science and individual heroism. Woman, more than man, delights in glory; it is, perhaps, that she does not examine so deeply as to see the motives and means, but looks at things in the aggregate or the result; she feels the national glow that would sink every thing at the thought of honour.

" While thy bold prows triumphant ride along
By trembling China, to the isles unsung
By ancient bard, by ancient chief unknown,
Till ocean's utmost shore thy commerce own."

Some of the conceptions in the Lusiad are noble; but honest critics tell us that we are much indebted to the translator of this work into English for our pleasure, the translation being superior to the original. This may be true, but, read as we have it, it is full of beauty and truth to those who see the country while they read the poem, though it must be confessed that there is nothing wonderfully original in the machinery. The poet copied Homer, Virgil, and Ariosto, after the manner of the schools; but his descriptions are natural, and that is enough. Although this is the epic of commerce, yet I believe that almost every other epic is read by merchants before the Lusiad.

It is surprising that commerce and letters should have been so long divorced, as it were; for they were once closely united. It was the Phenicians who diffused letters over Europe, while they were drawing wealth from the commerce of the world. The schools of the Hebrews flourished most when their commerce was at the highest prosperity. Letters have at all times been the necessary consequence of commercial enterprise, and from the days of De Gama the difficulties of the navigator have extended the science of astronomy and mathematics. These difficulties are so forcibly impressed upon the mind of the seaman, and indeed upon the mind of every one who trusts himself on the ocean, that I am surprised that any one would go a mile from land a second time without knowing enough of the science of navigation to find a port when he wished. Woman as I am, I never would sail another voyage without some knowledge of this science; enough to make ordinary calculations cannot lie very deep when so many pretend to it.

One great defect of the Lusiad was more owing to the laws of the schools than to the want of genius in the writer; this was a disposition to describe all the events, distances, escapes, &c., to the neglect of the natural world. Ichthyology, ornithology, conchology, and all natural history, were then beneath the epic standard. If these would have offended the critic of his day as not of sufficient importance, the voyager would now pardon him if he had descended to the description of the works of nature which were scattered around, and no doubt his copious mind was delighted with them all; but as he was writing an epic, he dared not interweave them with his verse. There is no want of feeling in the Lusiad, if there is of minute nature. Camoens was not a favourite of fortune; his name is added to those who live for others rather than for themselves. He had a just idea of the happiness of those minions of fortune who sail smoothly over

the sea of life, and find prosperous gales everywhere, and yet felt what he forcibly described of
the unfortunate man :

> " ——Through the dim shade, his fate casts o'er him
> A shade that spreads its evening darkness o'er
> His brightest virtues; while it shows his foibles,
> Crowding and obvious as the midnight stars,
> Which in the sunshine of prosperity
> Never had been descried."

It made me almost sick to think of poor Camoens's fate ; that one so talented, so learned, so
noble in his feelings, should have died so wretch-
edly, and found an ignoble grave.   I tried to con-
sole myself with the reflection that he had been
dead two centuries and a half, but could not ; for
where genius is impressed on the page, the immortal shade stands for ever before the reader.   There
is nothing of decay in the thought ; all is fresh and
blooming as it was before the ink was dry.   Em-
balmed by the tears of ages, a moving story grows
fresher by the lapse of time.   To a feeling heart
the meeting of Hector and Andromache was but
yesterday, and the wailings of Jephthah's daughter still sound in our ears.

Not half so much has been made of Southern
Africa and India as might have been made if
trade had been free and no monopolies known.
It is not only injurious but degrading to say you
must not buy here, or sell there, but under a
thousand restrictions.   The world should be
open for all, on equal terms ; the industry of all
should be regarded, and no particular set of men
ought to enjoy extraordinary privileges, nor any
nation be particularly favoured.   There are but
few places, thank Heaven, where an American
vessel cannot go. and but few indeed that they

have not visited. At home we females think but little of national glory, or rather not much of the means of supporting it ; but when abroad we become interested in every thing connected with commerce or naval power. A woman in these distant seas would be as proud to point to a fine frigate or a seventy-four from the United States as she would in dwelling on the fame of Washington, or any other distinguished man of our country. The feeling of nationality comes over us when abroad, but we leave it for others to support when we are at home. A female feels herself lost in the great mass of her countrywomen, but when abroad she represents them all ; and she must be dull indeed if she does not understand this situation. I was the first American woman who had visited some of the places I have described, and being a subject of curiosity, no one could be indifferent to such a situation ; it is not, however, to me a matter of vanity. Our men have been everywhere, but our women have not wandered much from home.

CHAPTER VII.

Departure from the Cape—Sight of St. Helena—Its Appearance
at Sea—Something of its History—Landing at St. Helena—
Its natural and other Productions—Its Appearance on Land
—Strength of the Place—Longwood—Tomb of Napoleon—
Reflections at his Grave—Fernandez Lopez—Comparison be-
tween St. Helena and Napoleon—Soothing Effect of the Sub-
limity of the Scripture—Recrossing the Equator—Calm at
Sea.

AFTER being well supplied with refreshments,
and putting every thing in tidy order, we sailed
on the 22d of March, and on the 28th we took
the south-east trade-winds, always so delightful
after they are settled, and on the 6th of April came
in sight of the island of St. Helena. As we approached this "prison-house in the sea," it appeared as a cloud in the heavens; but as you
come nearer it assumes a more solid looking form.
I gazed upon it until my imagination gave it
almost every shape that a cloud could assume,
from a whale to any thing monstrous, but never
like a weasel, excepting, as Polonius would say,
"it is black like a weasel." The next day we
anchored in front of Jamestown Valley. I had
ransacked all our books on board to get an account
of this wonderful island, intending to compare
their descriptions with my own observations. It
is unquestionably of volcanic origin, and was one
of the early productions of Omnipotence in those
seas, ages before man had ever navigated them.
It was discovered by the Portuguese, those pio-
neers of navigation, on St. Helen's day, the 21st

G

of May, 1501, and is about twelve hundred miles
from the continent, entirely detached from any
other island, reefs, or any thing but the mighty
Atlantic Ocean. It lies in latitude 5° 40′ south,
and longitude 15° 55′, west. In twelve years
after its discovery it was the residence of an ex-
iled Portuguese nobleman, who made some improvements in order to make it habitable. On
being restored to favour he returned to his country,
and in a few years the English examined it, but
did not think it worth possessing until after the
visit of Cavendish, in 1588, who made some additional improvements.   St. Helen, from whom it
was named, was the pious mother of Constantine
the Great ; and as Great Britain had not entirely
lost her partiality for saints, the name was not
changed.   The Dutch had possession of it for
several years before the English, but they did not
think it of sufficient importance to their commerce
to repay them for the cost they must be at to for-
tify and retain it.   Charles II. gave the island to
the East India Company.   It does not look half
so extensive as it is, probably from its great height,
rising, as it does, from the sea in an almost per-
pendicular wall, from six to twelve hundred feet ;
but it is more than ten miles long and six broad,
making not far from twenty-eight miles in circumference.   There are only four openings in the
great walls of this castle, and from these full-
mouthed batteries are pointed, and artillerists
standing by the guns with match in hand.   On
landing, we ascended by one of these openings
of nature, which, although strongly guarded, is
made more easy of ascent by art than one could
imagine from a distant view of it.

The valley is called James's Valley, and is a

fruitful spot. The fig, orange, date, and pome-
granate trees grow in great beauty here, and the
usual kitchen vegetables flourish abundantly.
The water is good, and can be made to irrigate
every part of the cultivated plains. The gum-
tree is still common on the island, although many
of them have been destroyed ; and the lofty cab-
bage-trees grow in great luxuriance, while the
willows seem to hang on the high grounds as
though they were clinging to the lowland brooks.
A great number of water-fowls hover around the
mountains, or coast near the walls in the sea.
The inhabitants once tried to cultivate wheat and
barley, but at length found it more profitable to
raise such articles as would more readily supply
the shipping which frequently call there on their
return from the India seas.

The place is as wonderful in its history as in
its situation, and was once nearly stocked by a
colony of those who were burnt out in London
in 1666, who in their desperation sought an asylum at St. Helena. James's Valley takes its name
from James II., after whom, also, the fort was
named. The town is in this valley, and has quite
a picturesque appearance. The churches, for
there are two, but only one parish, and the snug-
built houses perched so high in the air, and yet
low compared with heights still higher, give a fine
effect to the whole view. An elevated chain of
mountains divides the island into two unequal
parts ; but there are numerous ridges and valleys
of greater or less extent among these mountains.
Diana's Peak is the highest part of the island,
and commands a most superb prospect, for from
it you can see every thing on or about the island.
The ships look like small craft floating at the base

of this tremendous castle, and the albatrosses,
gulls, and other sea-birds, skimming half-way from
the sea to the height of Diana's Mountain, make
the whole a fine panorama ; one that nature does
not often in such vastness and magnificence afford.

What are great guns wanted for here? and yet
in every spot where a cannon can be placed, one of
large size is to be found. It would seem that if
only a common stone were thrown from these
towering battlements, it would sink a ship ; and
what could the navies of the world effect against
this castle?

A fine assortment of goods may be found in the
shops in this town, and there is much more cus-
tom here than one would imagine as he approached
the village. I bought several small articles, and
priced a number more, perhaps from curiosity.
There is a fine aqueduct leading the water for
more than a mile in extent, and which brings it
down conveniently for the shipping, who often
stop to replenish their water-casks, as well as their
fruit baskets. Great pains have been taken to
make good roads, and the success has been astonishing. Industry and perseverance, with wealth,
can almost work miracles. The cattle here, as
well as the sheep, are good. The air they breathe
is so pure, and their food is so sweet, that the beef
and mutton are better than in any other place in
the same latitude in the world. The poultry is
also very good : chickens and ducks were very
sweet and tender, and seemed to be in abundance. The people of St. Helena take great pains
to raise them for the use of the garrison, and
for the supply of ships that touch here. The
place, when I was there, seemed very healthy, yet
I did not see a very old person on the island, and
on inquiring, I could not find one verging towards

a hundred years of age; which is not an uncommon thing in our own country, where we suffer from every change of climate, from the extreme of heat to the extreme of cold. The air here, in the upper regions, is mild, not rising much above summer warmth, and the changes in the climate vary but a few degrees from one season of the year to another.

Longwood is on the north-east side of the island; it is a plain, raised seventeen hundred and sixty-two feet above the surface of the ocean, and abounds in vegetation of various kinds, but there are times when beef is high, when large India fleets arrive at the island. The birds are not so various or numerous as at other islands I have visited, but the canary is here, as in other places, a sweet songster. The canary is a delicate, yet often a hardy bird, and will live long and in good health if taken proper care of. In this island they are too common in the groves to be an object of attention among the tasteful; but it must be confessed, after all our discussions upon slavery, that a good canary-bird in a cage, educated by man, is a more beautiful singer than those who live in the retreats of nature. They may be taught from various instruments of music, and made to surpass nature by the assistance of art.

I had seen so much of natural scenery, and had so often attempted to describe it, that I should have visited St. Helena without emotion, notwithstanding all its wonders, if it had not been for the sentiments inspired by the place. This, it may easily be supposed, was the idea that the Emperor Napoleon was for several years confined here, and that his ashes were now entombed here.

There was something in this that seemed to ex-
aggerate the grandeur of the scene ; something
that gave it a deep and solemn cast ; that blended
the moral, historical, and wonderful with the
natural. When I first visited Longwood, I took
no more notice of the beauties of nature than I
should of the richness of the furniture in a room
where a dear friend was laid out for burial ; but
after a while, when my first impressions had sub-
sided, I could enjoy the beauties of the scene, as
well as contemplate the history of him whose
name has conferred immortality on this secluded
spot.

I sought the tomb of Napoleon. There was
an iron railing around a flat, dingy-coloured
stone, which was raised a few inches only above
the surface of the ground. A wooden railing
encloses the iron one, and within the former
three large willows overshadow the grave. We
marched up to the spot, took a twig of willow,
and ordered one of our attendants to bring us
some water from the spring whence the mighty
emperor drank daily. It was sweet water, and
as I drank, I thought of what old Cotton Mather
said in his works :—all the great virtues of cold
water will not be made known to us for a thousand years to come. It tasted sweeter to his
fevered lips than royal Tokay, or the still scantier
drops of the grapes of Shiraz.

As I bent over his grave, all the marvellous
events of his life came fresh into my mind. Born
on an island, he died on an island ; both birth-
place and burial-ground had been famous in
history, while he was more famous than all. I
saw him a spirited cadet ; then a proud subaltern ;
a general in Italy ; a commander in the Levant,

looking up to the Pyramids to catch glory from
their proud antiquity, and breathing it through a
sensitive French army. I followed him through
these fields of blood, until I saw him disperse the
corrupt legislature of France, and commence
what philosophers called the parallelism of the
sword ; his proud spirit growing still prouder
until all the crowned heads in Europe and the
world cowered and bowed before his august
presence. He was then in his saloon ; maps of
empires were before him, and he drew levies of
kingdoms as if in sport. I saw him placing the
diadem of France upon his brow, and still restless
until the iron crown of Italy was his also. Empires fell before him, as if fearful of his step, and
ambition took entire possession of his whole soul.
I then saw the magic thread of his destinies riven,
when he repudiated Josephine and became allied
to the house of Austria. The genius that had
guarded him to a hundred victories was capri-
cious in Spain, and deserted him at Moscow. At
Waterloo the destinies were against him, and his
fate was to die in this remote prison of the ocean,
and sleep under the humble stone which was
now before me.

That a man whose nod gave law to nations
should be at rest in this quiet little place seemed
to me indeed as a dream. It is a good place,
thought I, to reflect upon the value of human
life and the instability of fortune. My reflections
were made upon the stone itself, for I was enabled
to get within the railings and take a position
which few could enjoy. I made many inquiries
respecting his treatment while here, but the good
people were not inclined to say much about it.

I found, however, that Sir Hudson Lowe was not a favourite with them ; and my inferences, added to what I had heard, satisfied me that some little insults, to say the least, were offered him, but not from the people, for they now speak kindly of "General Bonaparte," who was liberal to all those allowed to approach him. He came to this place a fallen man ; and there was but little of that reverence the world pays to genius and greatness ever felt for him at St. Helena. The people were not so well pleased to think that their island would hereafter be considered as a prison.

Most of the people, I found, felt towards him as Byron did when he wrote—

> " Ill-minded man ! why scourge thy kind,
>   Who bow'd so low the knee ?
> By gazing on thyself grown blind,
>   Thou taught'st the rest to see.
> With might unquestion'd,—power to save,—
> Thine only gift hath been the grave
>   To those that worshipp'd thee ;
> Nor, till thy fall, could mortals guess
> Ambition's less than littleness !
>
> Thanks for that lesson !—it will teach
>   To after-warriors more
> Than high philosophy can preach,
>   And vainly preach'd before.
> That spell upon the eyes of men
> Breaks never to unite again,
>   That led them to adore
> Those pagod things of sabre-sway,
> With fronts of brass, and feet of clay.
>
> The triumph and the vanity,
>   The rapture of the strife—
> The earthquake shout of victory,
>   To thee the breath of life ;
> The sword, the sceptre, and that sway
> Which man seem'd made but to obey,
>   Wherewith renown was rife—
> All quell'd !—Dark spirit ! what must be
> The madness of thy memory !"

The house in which the emperor lived is now
converted to the uses of a granary or barn, and
I believe that there are horses stabled there ! but
whether this was accident, or pitiful design, I
could not discover ; it could not certainly have
been from any order of government, for they
built him a new and convenient house, to which
he would not remove. He felt that the death-fang
was on his heart, and that all would soon be over
with him. If he had not had a disease of the
breast, to which physicians give an anatomical
name, one was seated there that must have bowed
him to the grave sooner or later, and that was
disappointed ambition. To one who had never
felt the intoxication of power and dominion, and
whose bosom had no wounds of pride or con-
science, it would be hard to be confined in this
eagle's nest for many years, with the certainty
that there was no escape.

For several years after Napoleon came here it
is thought that he indulged hopes of being released, probably by some convulsion in Europe ;
but finding France quiet under the reign of the
Bourbons, and still at peace with England, he
lost all hopes, and the canker on his heart began
to increase in malignity, and to give strong prog-
nostics that he would die before his son should be
of age, or Europe would engage in a general war.
He was seldom heard to complain, but there was
a settled disdain upon his noble brow, and his lip
would curl with scorn as he beheld the proud
ships of his jailers passing to and from his
castle.

The conversations of Napoleon, which have
flooded the reading world, were, no doubt, in part
authentic as they came from his lips ; but it is

questionable whether he was indulging in his
own reveries, or sporting with the credulity of
his listeners. It is said that he seldom mentioned
his wife; whether he thought that she was wanting in affection in not offering to accompany him
in his exile, or whether he never had any affection for her, is not known. Those who analyze
the passions would perhaps say, that no two
mighty passions can exist at the same time in
any mind; ambition, they say, will destroy
avarice and love, and the latter has been known
to master both the others. All the communications he could make to his friends were verbal
ones; the eye of the police was too vigilant to
permit any others to escape from the island.

The good people of St. Helena are quite astonished at our enthusiasm for the character of Napoleon. They say "he was no friend to republics, nor
ever discovered any partiality to the people of the
United States; that he loved all the trappings
of royalty, and spurned every thing that did not
partake of aristocracy." Our only answer to this
was, that we neither feared nor hated him; and
that we could view him as a wonder in the history
of man; as something above the ordinary dimen-
sions of nature; a chastiser of nations, some of
whom deserved their chastisement; as a lover
and patron of the arts and sciences, and a protector of men of genius; as a destroyer of the
last remnants of the feudal system; and finally,
that many of us viewed him as an instrument in
the hands of God to promote unforeseen good to
men, as the two mighty Roman emperors paved
the way for the coming of the Messiah; and, in
short, that every thing great was intended by its

Maker for some great end. But after all, I was never entirely satisfied with my own excuse for my enthusiasm for this great man; and perhaps his noble physiognomy might have made a part of my admiration, for in every picture, or bust, or statue of Napoleon, whether young and spare, or grown older and corpulent, his countenance is one of the noblest ever formed.

To this sea-girt castle his name is not so dear as the exile who inhabited it more than three centuries ago. Fernandez Lopez had enjoyed wealth, fame, and power; but having lost all but honour, fled from the Indies to this retreat, and began to plant, and sow, and prepare it for the abode of his fellow-men. He bore his exile well, and after a few years his fortunes changed, and he came again into favour and prosperity. If all traces of his civilizing hand are now obliterated by deeper marks of improvement, still the contemporary of Columbus, and the philosopher in misfortune, is remembered as one of the benefactors of mankind.

We now took the fine road to Jamestown, about two miles and a half, and left St. Helena on Saturday, the 9th of April, steering north, with a delightful breeze. I kept my eyes directed towards the island, still thinking of the mighty dead. The place, on the whole, seemed in my mind a fit one for the tomb of Napoleon; for there was something analogous between St. Helena and himself. The mighty mass of stone was an instantaneous creation by volcanic power; and Napoleon arose at once by an eruption in the political and moral world. The French revolution threw him upward, and he bestrode the nations as a colossus. They had not done wondering at his fortunes when his reverses overtook him ; but sudden as was his elevation, his fame will last as long as the rock on which he lies. History has already placed him along with Cæsar and Alexander ; and if the grave philosopher shall in future times ask how much he has done for the world, and sarcastically add,

> " He left a name at which the world grew pale,
>   To point a moral, or adorn a tale ;"

still Napoleon will be a subject for young eyed wonder, and his deeds and his fate will furnish the schoolboy declaimer with matter for a thousand years to come ; and the historian, when he comes to his age—an age indeed of surpassing events—will kindle with some of the enthusiasm we now feel at the mention of his name.

St. Helena has become a resting-place for the ships which traverse the Indian Ocean, and it is said that not less than one hundred and fifty of them arrive there in a year. Those who visit this island will hereafter, as they have done ever since Napoleon's death, perform pilgrimages to his grave, as our classic travellers in Italy seek for the tombs of Cicero and Virgil.

Our minds after leaving a magnificent scene, or contemplating the achievements of a hero, experience a void that gives a restlessness to our spirits difficult to subdue. The best cure for these feelings that I could ever find when at sea was to survey the immensity of waters, or turn to some of the sublime or touching parts of the Scriptures. The contemplation of justice, mercy, and truth soothes and settles all our agitations;

and there is a beauty in holiness which, when we
become enamoured with it, occupies all our
heart, and absorbs all minor interests. As eternity is beyond time, so are these subjects beyond those that lie in our pathway through life.
There is something for ever so new in the Scriptures that no human mind can feel satisfied of having reached near their full meaning. Some new
thought will spring up in every text for contemplation. I do not believe there ever was a muti-
ny on board of a ship where the Bible was read
diligently by the whole crew. Works of fancy
and taste after a while grow tedious, from absorb-
ing too much of our attention at once, while the
Scriptures are not only interesting, but compel us
to direct our reasonings and views to ourselves.
If there ever was a book which could be called an
awakener of our own thoughts, it is that which
furnishes so many thoughts for us, the Bible. I
have read it where Christianity was professed,
followed, and held the highest claims to attention;
I have read it where superstition abounds, and
where infidelity, pagan infidelity, darkened the
whole land: it was the same heaven-illumined
page everywhere; but if ever peculiar glory
rested on it, it was when we were near those who
had never received its glad tidings, and who
never knew the true God.

On the 19th of April we crossed the equator,
but we were now all such old, experienced sailors
that Neptune did not think it worth while to pay
us a visit, nor did we expect him. If he had
come on board he would have found our stock
of liquor nearly the same as when he saw us before, except a little which had been used as medicine; and if he had brought his log-book, as sailors

playfully say he keeps, of all bad deeds done during his absence, I question whether he would
have found a single oath recorded, or one vile or
blasphemous expression set down to any one of
the crew of the Antarctic ; and, heathen as he is,
he would have been delighted to know how much
time they had devoted to reading the Bible.

We had now many calms or baffling winds.
There is nothing so distressing as a calm at sea.
Lying like a sleeping tortoise upon the water, the
vessel that in other times seems to partake of
life, now loses all animation ; or if there be a
slight motion, it is a sea-sickening sort of one.
The sailors are torpid, for it would be cruel to set
them at hard work under a tropical sun, and they
lie about as creatures without soul or spirit. In
such a situation the nights are restless, and the
days seem almost endless, although they are
only about equal in length to the nights. All
that memory can furnish, that books can supply,
or conversation offer, is nothing. Everybody
feels sick or dissatisfied, and you see yourself reflected in every face. You cannot laugh an hour
away ; and if you smile at all, you smile like
Cassius, who scorned his spirit that could smile
at any thing. If, gentle reader, you have an enemy, never wish him any thing worse than a calm
at sea. The sun seems to rise in wrath, and set
in fiery indignation, when one is under the equator, or near it, becalmed. Every thing was
changed but my husband's patience, which was
proof against all. He had before experienced the
evil, and had learned how to support himself under it. What must be the sufferings of those who
are in want of good and wholesome water at such
times ? We, thanks to Heaven, had a good sup-

ply of both water and provisions; and still these calms were dreadful.   The tales of distress which we have read at such times, however horrid, were, I believe, only half told.   The inhabitants of Judea never panted for rain as we did for wind, when the prophet prayed for it and the little cloud arose.   At length, on the 13th of May, we took the north-east trade-winds, and were wafted along so sweetly for eighteen days, when we arrived at Tercera, that the whole time seemed hardly as long as one of those days in the calm.

CHAPTER VIII.

The Azores—Climate and Soil—Volcanic Origin—Liberia—
Character of that Colony—Lot Cary—Effects of Exploring
Expeditions—Missionary Societies—The bad Effects of In-
toxicating Liquors—Indians unacquainted with Intemperance
until taught by Europeans—Course that should be pursued
by Missionaries—Intellectual Character of the Indians—Their
Ferocity ascribed to Ignorance and Ill-treatment—Arrival at
Cadiz—Disappointment in not being allowed to Land—Slight
Sketch of its History—The Cholera—Notice of it in New-
York.

TERCERA is one of the Azores, which group
is nine in number ; some writers make more of
them, by taking into the account some large rocks,
but there are only nine islands of consequence,
the principal one of which is called Tercera,
measuring twenty-five miles in length, fifteen in
breadth, and about fifty-four in circumference, the
figure being, of course, rather elliptical than cir-
cular. This group lies in the Atlantic Ocean,
about 36° to 40° north latitude, and from 25° to 35°
west longitude. The Portuguese took possession
of these islands in about 1446 ; some historians
fix the date earlier and some later, and no precise
time can be fixed for their discovery or possession.
In former ages nature appears to have been at
work in raising islands by volcanic power; but in
later days she seems to have lost her vigour, or is
disposed to quit her labours, for no island of importance has been thrown from the deep beds of

ocean for the cultivation of man since the discovery of these islands by the Portuguese. The soil is productive, and oranges and grapes grow in great profusion. The climate is healthy, and though earthquakes sometimes terrify the inhabitants, still it is seldom that they cause any essential injury. It is the opinion of some philosophers that these islands are supported by volcanic arches, whose vast ovens are burning with perpetual fires; this is no very comfortable thought for those who keep it in mind, but the inhabitants here think this the garden of the world, or at least the place where it might be made; and it is most assuredly true that a finer climate can hardly be found than that of the Azores. The government, though arbitrary, is mild, and I could find no instances of oppression. These islands were once supposed to belong to Africa, by geographical position, but of late years they have been classed as European, for it is certain that the new race of inhabitants are Portuguese. Portugal has always held them in affection, because they were first known to them in modern times, and have been constantly under the protection of that government.

The whole island of Tercera, as far as I could see it, and we made frequent tours into the country, is but an exhausted volcano. So far as I have seen the islands of the sea through more than three hundred degrees of longitude, they appear to have been brought forth by volcanoes in the oceans of the east and west. It is true that they are at work now, but they must have been more active in former times than at present.

The Portuguese here are a quiet and inoffensive

people, but they are hardly acquainted with the
growth of our country; they still think that we
are in our infancy, as they measure all growths by
length of years. They had heard of our settlement on the coast of Africa, and spoke of it as a
feeble attempt to get rid of our surplus black
population; they think it will not last long, but
we indulge in other hopes ; and I feel persuaded
that this is one of the most important colonies
ever planted since the settlement of North America. Its climate is as healthy as any we have
ever known, notwithstanding the location. The
settlement has flourished as well, and is increasing as fast, as did any of the American colonies,
and their commerce is greater in proportion to
the number of inhabitants. None are more attentive to the cultivation of mind and morals, and
their territory is unbounded, for the tenth part of
Africa is not at present under cultivation. Most
of this fifth part of the globe is wild as it was
when the beasts of the field and birds of the air
were its lords-proprietors. I can see nothing to
prevent this colony from being the nucleus of
nations; flourishing in arts and sciences, in commerce, in civil freedom, and all that constitutes a
state. What can be more rational than these
noble efforts to advance the interests of man,
particularly degraded man ? My nation and
people are now doing something to wipe off a
dark spot from their escutcheon.

If this colony is cherished, the United States
will reap the advantages of it; they will get rid
of their surplus population of blacks, and at the
same time be planting a colony from whence
great commercial results may be expected. I con-

ceive that there is to be a change in a great portion of the globe, and that change will take place speedily.   The agents and governors of the colonization society have been men of talents and perseveranc : the most remarkable man, however, among them, was an African.   The Rev. Lot Carey, who died not long since at Monrovia, was an extraordinary man.   While he was a slave in Virginia, by his own industry and anxiety for knowledge, he learned to read and to write, and acquired so much general information that he was intrusted with the management of a large tobacco warehouse.   In this business, by his perquisites and his industry in the time allowed him, he accumulated a sufficient sum of money to purchase, not only his own freedom, but that of his wife and children also.   He was discreet, sober, and religious, and became a preacher of the gospel while yet a slave.   Many who heard his discourses thought his views of the Bible were excellent. When the colonization society was formed, and Liberia purchased, he was ready at the commencement of the settlement to depart with the earliest settlers, and took his share in every labour.   He acted not only as a spiritual guide, but as a civil magistrate, and as deputy agent, and for a while, in the absence of Mr. Ashman, as chief magistrate of Liberia.   In every situation which he was called to fill, he not only evinced the high powers of a gifted mind, but the pure spirit of a righteous man.   If such specimens of intellect and virtue can be found rising up among slaves, what may we not expect from these people in a state of civil and religious freedom, enlightened by schools in every branch of knowledge ?

This must be effected by exploring expeditions,

by missionary societies, and by a universal temperance, which is rapidly pervading the whole
population of the globe. These exploring expeditions should be got up by individual enterprise,
assisted by government. Their failure the government will not be answerable for, but their success must of course be a national benefit. According to the present law of nations, discovery
gives the right of possession, so far as it relates
to any other power than the aborigines ; if this
should be considered of consequence, certainly the
trade of lands discovered would for some time be
of advantage to our commercial people. It were
well, too, that we should do something for the
world whose commerce we enjoy ; we have now
a name to support, and what have we done to
raise its glory ? Our whalers have done something worthy of remembrance, but this is all. To
Nantucket, New-Bedford, Stonington, and a few
other places, is most of the credit due for all the
discoveries we have made in the Pacific Ocean.
These enterprising men have traversed every sea
in search of whales, and they have generally
communicated to the world what they have found
new or profitable. When the government has
wanted information, they have been ready to communicate it from their very accurate and satisfactory journals ; if no advantage has been taken
of their discoveries, it is not their fault.

The next step to finding where savage men live
is that of furnishing them the means of instruction; and this can only be done by sending enlightened missionaries to teach them civilization and
Christianity. Wherever an intelligent missionary establishment is to be found, there good results have been witnessed, notwithstanding the

abuse of some, and the fear of others; there is no exception to the rule. Civilized nations have heretofore carried intoxicating liquors to those they visited, and while they opened up the light of mind and religion to them, have taught them the vices found in corrupt associations of the civilized world. The poor wretches had acquired all the vices before they had been taught to practise a single virtue that they had not before known; thus civilization has heretofore been to them a curse instead of a blessing. But now it is otherwise; the refinements of society are taught them without its vices.

Ardent spirits have in general been an article of traffic in these regions, and the poor wretches have been cheated by proffering to their lips the intoxicating draught. It is the sweet recollection of our little voyage that we have never offered to the lips of primitive man one drop of ardent spirits; we have met them and drunk the waters of their springs, and never said to them that there was any thing that an Indian would like better. I never saw an Indian inebriated, because we never gave him any thing to steal away his senses. It has been, as far as I am informed, the universal practice to carry ardent spirits to the people of these rude islands, and the baneful effects no one ever doubted while engaged in the traffic. Why should it not be made a penal, as it is a moral, offence to teach them drunkenness? There is a new and a better era to come than has as yet been known; for even the pilgrims of New-England gave the aborigines these strong waters in traffic. The visiters to these benighted regions should never let them

know that such a thing as a drunken man ever
existed. It is said by some that they already
have inebriating draughts among them; but this
is true only to a certain extent, and that a very
small one. They seldom make use of narcotics,
or of any thing that entirely destroys their senses.
The process of distillation they are unacquainted
with, and but few simple juices are very inebriating. Of all the natives unaccustomed to
Europeans, I never saw one who had any marks
of intemperance about him. Travellers may say
what they please of these natives in regard to intemperance, but they never bear any of the marks
of it until they become acquainted with civilized
man. The ava-root and other narcotics produce a stupefaction, but they leave no blotch,
no laxity of muscle, no disgusting redness of the
eyes, and all the wretched symptoms induced by
the use of ardent spirits.

Missionaries, who should be at first school-
masters, and then preachers, should be sent to
every isle of the sea as well as to the continent.
Letters should be first taught, with domestic arts;
and then the high principles of morality and religion. If day-schools for children, and Sun-
day-schools for men, women, and children,
should be established, I firmly believe that the
work of refinement and morals would go rapidly
on in any of those islands which we have visited,
and which are now in darkness. The natural
capacity of these savages, I believe, is not inferior
to that of any people in the world. It is, I think,
—I go to no theorist for the doctrine,—a law of
nature, that wherever there is a fine physical or-
ganization among mankind, there mental capacity
will be found also. This may be a mortifying

doctrine to proud man in the old clans, tribes, or
nations, but it is nevertheless true. I believe
there is as much genius in some of the islanders
we saw as can be found in France, England, or
America. These new regions hardly ever see

" The tenth transmitter of a foolish face ;"

but the natives are quick of perception in all the
ordinary duties of life, and are also acute observers of passing events ; they compare and
combine most rapidly in every instance where
they are called upon to act. I do not believe that
He who made man has given any particular gifts
to any one race. If there be any superiority, it is
in giving to some of the islanders we saw a larger
corporeal frame than to any race of men which
history has ever enumerated. The progress of
the improvement of these people depends on us ;
and we shall be answerable in future for the intelligence and virtue they shall possess. Much
may be done at a little expense, for there are persons of good education who are willing to settle
at these places if they could have the protection
of government and the assistance of the charita-
ble in their exertions. The English will in a few
years be the language of all the islanders where
English or American missionaries are established;
for as soon as the natives become more enlightened, they will find that their own scanty language will be insufficient to express their ideas ;
and picking up a little English from common intercourse with those who have come
teach them, they will be anxious to gain something more from day to day until they become
proficients in English literature. They are,

as I have said, imitative, and of course soon learn
to write well ; the chirography of Pomaré, which
has been shown in the United States, was elegant—such as a professor of penmanship might
be proud of. The missionaries are, at least all
that I have seen, satisfied with the quickness and
assiduity of the natives, and also with their do-
cility when they become impressed with the idea
that they are receiving some benefit from instruction, and that their teachers have no other object
than to do them good. The missionaries should
have nothing to do with trade ; that must be left
to others ; for if these people once get the idea into
their heads that the missi naries are labouring to
gain wealth, that moment their influence is at an
end, and their only protection will be a resort to
arms. It is not from a sanguinary disposition
that the natives make attacks on vessels that visit
them, but from a desire to obtain what others have
at the easiest rate.

On the 10th of June we arrived at Cadiz. The
harbour is a noble one ; the city is one of the
finest in Spain, and, if properly garrisoned, must
be capable of sustaining an obstinate defence.
I make these observations, begging the reader
to understand that I know, or think I do, which
is perhaps of quite as much importance, a good
deal about the subject of defence, from hearing an almost perpetual conversation about the
capability of defence of one place or another in
parts of the world where there were no guns or
castles, as well as in those which were strongly
fortified. In this bay rode the proud navies of
Spain in every age of Spanish greatness, from the
invincible armada to the time Villeneuve sailed to
be beaten at the battle of Trafalgar. This was
the rendezvous of the navies of the New World,

The Earl of Essex, the favourite of Queen Elizabeth, took this city in 1596; it has sustained several sieges, but was taken by the French in a late period of history. It is an old city, and no doubt is full of those things that interest a traveller whose views are directed to objects less superficial than those which strike the eye of the common observer. Our tastes change with our experience : at first we look at whatever stands most prominent, such as great and magnificent buildings, or striking peculiarities of the people ; but we afterward direct our attention to more minute matters, which do not lie on the surface, and in all probability find more satisfaction in these researches than in gazing at what everybody sees, or has examined. But I was deprived of the pleasure of describing this city, as we were not permitted to stay there. This was at first surprising to me, for I could not conceive of any cause why I should not see the people of Cadiz ; and I grieved the more at it, as I had informed my female friends at Manilla that I was to visit Cadiz, and therefore was under various commands from them to some of their friends in the city. We were not permitted to stay in the port when it was known that we had come from Manilla many months before, and that the cholera was there ; our journals, also, showed that two of our men had died of this disorder. The authorities were very peremptory on this point, and threatened to fire into us if we did not depart instantly. This was silly as it was timid and arbitrary ; for after so many months, if the disease had been contagious we were free from any infection, and could not have communicated it to the people of Cadiz. When we bring matters home to us,

H

how much better do we reason than when our remarks are general. How ridiculous were these quarantine laws to us, who had been out of danger over the distance of nearly fifteen thousand miles of ocean ! Not having a single man sick of any contagious disease, nor of any other, except accidental indisposition, we were forced to leave this port without discharging a particle of cargo, and to direct our course to Bordeaux. The sickness called the cholera, it is true, had been on board of our vessel, and carried off two of the crew, but those who early made known their sickness to my husband and myself were cured ; these two were beyond assistance when we were informed of their sickness.

This disease did not then appear in my eyes as it since has. I considered it entirely an Asiatic disorder, and one that would be confined to that country. It had passed from the Hoogly and the Ganges to Manilla, and was fatal among the lower classes of society, but was by no means confined to them ; still the higher classes in Manilla thought so little of it, or rather, perhaps, said so little about it, that I did not think much of its deadliness. The mortality among our sailors was less than usual, and therefore their deaths by this disease made no very deep impression on my mind. It was only after we were denied the hospitalities of Christians that I began to reflect on the selfishness of people in their fear of an epidemic.

I was aware that this sweeping disorder had entered Europe by way of Astracan, and had been very deadly, but little did I think it would ever spread over my own dear country ; causing so great a panic that for nearly a mile in the principal street of New-York, at noonday, not half a dozen people could be seen. Desolation had extended over all my native city; and while looking over my journal to prepare it for publication, every hour the house was filled with bulletins of the progress of this mighty scourge of mankind. The different symptoms and the different treatment were sufficient to distract every one. It was difficult to know what course to pursue when a person was attacked; and until the disease was far advanced, it was almost impossible to tell whether the patient was sick with it or not. The symptoms were almost as various as the patients; cramps, diarrhœa, and occasional spasms are general premonitions of the disease; no headache or dizziness marks its coming on, but rather, like the apoplexy, its forerunner was a high state of animal spirits. I never left New-York during the whole time it was raging in the city, and had an opportunity of witnessing its disorganizing effects on society, as well as the sufferings of those whom it has attacked. The deaths were numerous, and the disease came as a thief at night; but the disease, and even the deaths, were nothing to the alarm. This spread through all circles, and seemed to be a disease of itself, more malignant than the cholera. The constituted authorities did much, and the rich subscribed large sums of money, but if individuals in common life had not made exertions, personal and pecuniary, the sufferings would have been more intense than they were. Such sweeping calamities have a sad effect in many instances on the human mind; they dry up all the generous currents of the heart, and destroy all the wholesome ceremonies of burial and funeral honours. Although there are frequently unne-

cessary expenses attending a funeral, yet there is
something dreadful in having a friend die in such
a manner as to be hurried to the grave as a vile
suicide who had no objects or wishes to live for. To
have a being whom we love this hour well—sick
the next—dead the next—and hurried to the grave
before his ashes are cold—is too much for human
nature. I believe if every one was obliged to
live in the city during the rage of the sickness,
that many evils would be avoided. The natural
ties between the rich and the poor and the middle
classes of society would not be sundered ; one
could give relief to others, and all, depending on
Heaven, would go on as usual in most things.
The great evils of this disease have sprung from
alarms ; fear has slain more than disease itself.
In future days the folly of flying from the cholera
will be evident to all, and the great mass of the
inhabitants of every city will come to the truth
with the fact—

" I ran from trouble, and trouble ran and overtook me."

All the individual miseries which have flowed
from the cholera will never be known. The tears
and prayers of widows and orphans have had their
influence with the God of mercies, and another
scourge may not, perhaps, overtake them. This
disease has touched the rich, but it has dwelt with
the poor ; it does, indeed, sweep off vice, but it
does not keep always with the vicious ; the temperate, the abstemious, the cautious, and even the
extremely scrupulous have fallen victims to its
ravages. " *Be ye ready*" is a maxim for all who
live among men,

CHAPTER IX.

On the 20th of June we arrived at Bordeaux, which lies in longitude 0° 34' west, and latitude 44° 50' 13" north, and is the chief city of the department of the Gironde. It is built on the left bank of the River Garonne, that is, the left bank after military language, which I have discovered is different from naval usage. Military men speak as going down a river, and naval as sailing up. In consideration of the loyalty of this city, Louis XVIII. built a bridge across the river, which is seven hundred feet in length and is thrown into seventeen arches, and has a fine appearance. This was the first time I ever had an opportunity of visiting what might be called an ancient city. Those I had seen did not exceed three hundred years in age ; this was founded so early that the precise age of it is not known. It was known to the Romans in the days of Cæsar, and in the fifth century it was taken by the Goths in their sweeping march of destruction. It was destroyed after this by the Normans, but as it was a convenient place for commerce it soon rose again from its desolation, and was considered as an important city. It came into the hands of Louis VII. by his marriage with the daughter of the Duke of Guienne. The king was soon divorced from his wife, and she reserved the city and country around; but in 1152 she married the Duke of Normandy, who afterward became King of England. The antiquarians here pretend to show the precise spot where the King of France, when he was made prisoner by the Black Prince, was confined for more than ten years. In a few years after the memorable feats of the Maid of Orleans, the city was restored to France; and in about a century after this, it was nearly destroyed by a rebellion of the people on account of some arbitrary taxation upon salt, which article was much used there for preserving their provisions for vessels. It was a place of great consequence to France, and was protected in its commerce by the Bourbons, and in gratitude remained true to the royal cause during the revolution of 1789, for which it was severely punished by the furious republicans of that day. They were the last to yield to the revolutionists, and the first to hail the restoration of the Bourbons, when they returned from their long exile. The city has all the marks of antiquity about it; there are some pieces of masonry there that probably were laid before the Christian era. The number of inhabitants is probably not greater than it was a thousand years ago—not exceeding one hundred thousand. To an American the walls give the place a heavy appearance. There are nineteen gates in these walls, and every thing about it looks as though, in former days, the inhabitants were capable of making a formidable resistance, particularly before the invention of gunpowder. The suburbs of the city are delightful residences. The inhabitants are nearly all Catholics, there being forty-six Catholic churches and but one Protestant in the city ; some of these edifices are noble buildings, though they are not all in the best repair. Bonaparte built a palace here about the time of his Austrian alliance, perhaps rather to conciliate the people than with an intent of residing in it any considerable portion of his time. He wished to eradicate from the hearts of the people all affection for the Bourbons, and one way of effecting this was to display the munificence of the new government. This was not bad policy, but proved of no avail ; the attempts he made to benefit France, and they were not a few, were all destroyed by his Spanish and Russian wars, in which the elements fought against him as well as men. The harbour is well protected by forts, and looks much more lively with the shipping of all countries than the city does ; and to me the most cheerful sight was that of the American flag flying more frequently than that of any other nation but that of France. To one long from home it sends a summer feeling to the heart to see the flag of our country, long respected for the enterprise of our merchants, but now for the glory of our victories. I rejoiced that this flag had not only been consecrated by bravery, but commemorated by the muse ; and I could not refrain from repeating, as I saw it waving from the tall masts of some of our noble vessels, a few lines of one of the poets of my native city :

> " Flag of the seas !   On ocean's wave,
>   Thy stars shall glitter o'er the brave,
>   When death, careering on the gale,
>   Sleeps dankly round the bellied sail.

And frighted waves rush wildly back
Before the broadside's reeling rack.
The dying wanderer of the sea
Shall look, at once, to heaven and thee;
And smile to see thy splendours fly
In triumph o'er his closing eye.

Flag of the free heart's only home!
    By angel hands to valour given,
Thy stars have lit the welkin dome,
    And all thy lines were born in heaven!
For ever float that standard sheet!
    Where breathes the foe that stands before us,
With freedom's soil beneath our feet,
    And freedom's banner streaming o'er us!"

This is part of an old ode written while the war
fever was upon us: to have made it perfect the
writer should have seen that flag made glorious in
the bosom of peace, as it then floated before me.

The whale-fishery is carried on here, but the
commanders of these whale-ships are mostly
Americans, as in fact are the seamen. An American whale-ship is a little empire, and generally
one of the best regulated ones. Every one has a
share in the profits, and his fortune and reputation
are at stake. This works wonders; no people
are more hardy than these men, and none have
been more prosperous in their business. I was
sorry to hear that the sand was accumulating at
the mouth of this harbour, but as human ingenuity is now busy to find out some remedy for
such evils on both sides of the water, I trust it will
be one of no great continuance.

The museum is large, but did not abound with
as many curiosities as I expected from its age.
The library of the Academy of Sciences was the
largest I had ever seen. There were some
splendid editions, but not many in comparison

with the whole number of volumes. The academy of the deaf and dumb is in good repute, but I had no opportunity of seeing a display of the pupils. In every part of the city there is something of the bustle of business, but more particularly at the gates opening towards the river; but these places are not much visited by ladies. I went to the church of St. Bernard to see the tomb of Montesquieu, who was born in the neighbourhood of this city, and buried here. The French have a great reverence for his memory, and from the enthusiasm with which they speak of him, one would think he was some Lord Byron or Thomas Moore, who had written poetry until every lady's head was turned with it. My companions could not inform me what he had written, but only that he was admired by every good Frenchman. At length I found his book on the Spirit of the Laws, in English; and as far as I could judge, he deserved the reputation of a great man: but I still wonder how he came to be admired by the French ladies, except because it is a fashion among them to admire great men. I wish this was the fashion in our own country, but I fear that thousands of our New-York ladies pass by Trinity churchyard, in Broadway, without knowing that a greater man than Montesquieu has a monument there: the monument of one of whom it might be said—

" When on a rock which overhung the flood,
And seemed to totter, commerce shivering stood ;
When credit, building on a sandy shore,
Saw the sea swell, and heard the tempest roar ;
Heard death in every blast and in each wave,
Or saw, or fancied that she saw, her grave ;
When property, transferred from hand to hand,
Weakened by change, crawled sickly through the land ;

н 3

When mutual confidence was at an end,
And man no longer could on man depend ;
Oppressed with debts of more than common weight,
When all men feared a bankruptcy of state ;
When, certain death to honour and to trade,
A sponge was talked of as our only aid ;
That to be saved we must be more undone,
And pay off all our debts by paying none ;
Our Country's better genius, born to bless
And snatch our sinking credit from distress,
Didst thou step forth, and, without sail or oar,
Pilot the shattered vessel safe to shore."

The present Archbishop of Bordeaux, John
Cheverus, was for many years an inhabitant of
the United States.   During the reign of terror,
in 1793, being then a young Catholic priest, he
fled to England, and from thence embarked for
the city of Boston, in company with a very esti-
mable man, much his senior, the Rev. Dr. Mattignon.   In Boston these priests built up a flock,
and were in the way of doing much good.   When
a bishop of Boston was necessary for the Catholic
church, Dr. Mattignon urged that his young friend
should be appointed in preference to himself.   As
bishop he became the most popular man in that
city among all denominations.   He was on good
terms with every sect of Christians ; he was not
only polite, affable, and kind, but was unceasing
in doing, wherever he was called to labour, among
the sick or the poor ; nor were his exertions confined to these ; he was the confidant of many in
the higher circles of life in all denominations ;
probably no man ever lived in Boston more
generally beloved.   After twenty-seven years' labour in the United States, he was appointed by
Louis XVIII. Bishop of Montauban, and requested
to leave the United States as soon as possible.   At
first he declined the appointment, preferring to

live in his own humble way in Boston to changing
it for the parade of a bishop's life in France, but
the request being repeated, as it is said, by the king
himself, and his health not being good, he came to
the determination of leaving America for France.
The separation from his old flock, and from his
other friends, was painful indeed. When he
reached Montauban, the Protestants vied with the
Catholics to do him honour. He hailed them all
his friends, and was ready to do them any service
in his power. He had soon an opportunity
to show some further traits in his character.
There was a great freshet, which caused the
rivers near Montauban to overflow their banks
and endanger the lives of the farmers. He
called all the active spirits of the city together, put
himself into the smallest boat, and led the way to
assist those in jeopardy. He brought hundreds
of them to the city, opened his palace, and lodged
and fed them until the waters had abated. Not
content with this, he sent men to save the cattle
and other property of the dismayed inhabitants,
so that, through his firm and generous conduct,
but little loss was sustained. The king, hearing
of this, and knowing that his finances were not
in a very flourishing condition, sent him a very
considerable sum of money, of which, however,
he did not retain a cent, but distributed the whole
amount among those who had suffered the most
by the flood and had the least left. His fame
was so generally known, that when the old Archbishop of Bordeaux died he was appointed, as
it were by universal acclamation, to fill his
place. He was then made by Charles X. a peer
of France. This office was not given to him
because he wished it, but the king thought

he would bring a good share of influence into
the chamber of peers. It was known that he
was a well-read civilian, and watched the progress of the institutions of the people of the
United States with great care; but I believe he
never took an active part as a politician, for his
whole soul was in his religious duties. It is
seldom that an archbishop preaches, but he set
the example to his higher clergy by preaching
and exhorting often. While we were at Bordeaux his liberal views in politics and religion
were often spoken of; not that he was ever suspected of a want of sincerity in his attachment
to his religion, but he had charity for all mankind.
Like Fenelon, he only wished to do good, having
no desire to accumulate wealth. His charities
to the poor were great, and he assisted in every
improvement of the city. That he was not ambitious was the opinion of all Bordeaux, for they
said that he had refused to accept the office of
tutor to the young Duke of Bordeaux, then heir-
apparent to the throne. This was considered in
France the highest honour that could be given
to any subject—that of forming the mind of him
who was to reign; it was, as they think, in
some measure reigning himself: but this he
had no desire to do. It could be plainly seen
when we were there, that there was a gloom on
the face of the good bishop, for he could not be
ignorant of the state of the public mind in Paris,
and some symptoms of a revolution appeared
even in the loyal city of Bordeaux. In a few
days after our departure the revolution broke out
in Paris which hurled Charles X. from the throne,
and called in a citizen king. In this change of
affairs the bishop lost his peerage, as did all

others made by Charles; but this was no cause
of grief to the good man; it gave him an opportunity to devote his whole time to his ecclesias-
tical duties. It would have been fortunate for
the young duke if he had had such a guardian
and instructer as Bishop Cheverus. If Charles
X. had been instructed by a wise, prudent teacher
of the nature and feelings of man, he would not
have lost his crown.

France is a delightful country, and under a
mild government would be a happy one. Everybody strives to be as happy as they can in France;
it is not always so with us; among some of our
people there is a disposition to look at things on
the dark side. If we hear of the approach of a
comet, it disturbs the peace of some who are not
wanting in good sense in other things; but the
approach of a comet in France would only produce a pleasant sensation, and they would draw
no unfavourable auguries from it, but only envy
the scientific the pleasure they would find in
watching its progress through the heavens.
There is such ease in the manners of the French, so
much of habitual politeness, and such a desire to
make you happy, that one is unwilling to leave
the society to be found almost anywhere in
France.   The agriculture of the country, it is said,
is in a prosperous state; there is a neatness about
some of their fields and vineyards that is delightful to one accustomed to ruder culture.   The
cultivators of the soil own much more of it than
the same class of people did before the revolution.
It seemed to me almost impossible that this could
be the people that only a few years ago—a few in
the age of a nation—had suffered so much by revo-
lutionary fury; a people whose fathers, sons, and

brothers fell by the dagger of the assassin or under
the bloody guillotine. There were no traces of
misery now,—nothing to remind you that such
scenes of horror had ever passed, except now and
then the mark of a cannon-ball in some old
house, and these ruins are not numerous. From
reading all the agonizing details of the revolution,
I expected to find many insane wretches, made
so by these sufferings : but after all my inquiries—
and I made them until they created a smile,—I
could not find a single maniac whose madness
could be traced to witnessing or sharing in these
horrors. How soon a generation is forgotten !—
even that great wonder of men, Napoleon, whose
name was on every tongue from one end of the
earth to the other, was now seldom mentioned
in the city, or anywhere in France. What a lesson to those who seek fame through fields of
devastation and blood !

In Bordeaux I found a file of American newspapers. It was true that they contained nothing
new or interesting to most readers ; but to me
they were dear as the light that visited my eyes.
There were the little squabbles of editors ; the
complaints of some neglected actors, the puffs
required to vend patent medicines, or to call
the attention to a sale of the last importation of
bonnets or fans. All was delightful to me, for I
knew that the interesting Mr. A—— was to preach
in —— street, on a particular evening, and that
the learned Dr. M—— would give a lecture on
such an evening on political economy, or on
steam-engines, or internal improvements, or on
the raising of hemp, or the last public sale of domestic manufactures. This medley was delightful. I could rejoice at the hymeneal register, and
drop a tear over the obituary notices. The exile

never kissed the ground on his return to his native land with more enthusiasm than I read these newspapers ; only some fifty days old. To me they seemed as thrown on the breakfast-table all wet from the press. I read all the advertisements, as delicious morsels of information ; not a word was omitted. The speeches of politicians at dinners given for their political services were read with attention, in truth devoured. It made not a cent's difference on which side they spoke, for they were my countrymen, and they had a right to differ among themselves ; nor was I sure I wished them to agree if they found more pleasure in disputing? I felt no disposition to set them right if I could have had the power given me, for I did not know who was right, but thought them all so. The number of new publications I saw advertised was such that it seemed as if all that my countrymen had been doing while I was absent had been to cultivate their minds ; and I was happy to find that they had enjoyed themselves in this way. I expected to find every one so improved that I should hardly dare to see my old friends. I learned the "whereabouts" of all the state and general government politicians, and what they had been saying and doing in my absence.

I picked up a few American books in this city, of recent date, and these were greeted as old friends, and read with delight ; but I made no criticisms, for one long absent from home never complains of any thing from that quarter. I could wish that all who criticise their own people were obliged to wait before they commenced their review until they had got three or four thousand miles from home, and I really think we should have much

less vituperation. If any writer of distinction
could see his works in distant countries, and know
what ubiquity he possesses, he must be happy
indeed if he is conscious that what he has written
is not exceptionable on the score of principle.
Irving, Cooper, Webster, and several of our poets
are found at many places we visited; and those
and other American names were familiar in Asia
and Africa as well as in Europe. I must say,
however, that English vessels are more likely to
bring out recent literary and scientific productions than our own, but do not equal us in
general in the extent of the useful library made
up for the voyage. Hardly a single vessel thinks
of putting to sea for a long voyage without
taking several hundred volumes. Master mariners have found out that officers and men on
a long voyage can do their duties, and have some
time to improve their minds too. The selection
is often not the best that might be made for this
purpose, particularly of books relating to our
own country, for there are but few who visit
other countries that know much about our own.
It would be doing a service, if some one acquainted
with books were to make out a catalogue of
such as should be collected for ordinary and for
long voyages. All the approved naval journals
and voyages are indispensable as guides for the
purpose of obtaining the most information in the
shortest time. Some good commercial dictiona-
ries, and geographies, and gazetteers should be
always at hand ; and works of taste should not
be forgotten. An interesting work appears with
double charms on shipboard. The mind is then
concentrated, and cannot be dissipated by amuse-
ments or trifles—it comes with all its force to a

subject. Not only a matter of taste but a moral lesson sinks deeper in the mind when there is nothing to distract our attention. The great mathematician of our country, who is considered greater in Europe than in America, gained most of his information during voyages at sea. His name and his commentaries on La Place's great mathematical work are familiar to all men of science in France. Dr. Bowditch performed many long voyages, as factor and master, from the United States to India ; always having with him good officers, he had leisure to go through those long and difficult calculations which have laid the foundation of his great fame, so valuable and so dear to his country. Every person at sea is constantly reminded of him, as his Navigator is on every officer's table. This book, I believe, has taken the place of all others among our mariners, and is highly esteemed by navigators of other countries. It is said, also, that the numerous corrections made in tables by him were made at sea. I am surprised that tales or poetry are not often written at sea, for passengers surely have leisure when officers have no spare time. The inspiration is generally from the pure air, which, after all, is one of the best inspiring agents in nature. The dreams of Delphos were upon some divine afflatus, as the poets call it, which were probably nothing more than a sweet bracing wind.

I was delighted at the information I received here, that my countrymen were much respected in France, and that we were no longer considered an infant nation, but as one that bore a proud flag, that had reared and was rearing historians, poets, orators, and above all a class of profound statesmen to guide the vessel of state. I had not

thought much of these things when I left my
native land, but now I was identified with all of
them in some degree; certainly in feeling, if
nothing more. I looked forward to the day when
my own dear boy might be an active man among
them, and the prospective view of that period,
generally long to those who have children, did
not seem to me at this moment half so long
as I had been absent from my country and my
child. Travellers, it is said, are mostly short
lived, and I can easily conceive of the truth of
the remark, for they suffer and enjoy so much
that the human frame is exhausted by the various
emotions of excitement—from anxiety, from gratifying news, and all the changes that agitate their
hearts. In the midst of these emotions I thought
I should sit down in my own chamber, and enjoy,
oh! sweetly enjoy all my former domestic quiet;
and yet I would not give up the memory of the
things I have seen, suffered, and enjoyed, to be
sure of the most protracted existence. Such con-
tradictions we are, and such we shall always remain. The distance from home now was a mere
trifle; only three thousand miles, and that the
Atlantic, my own ocean, for it washed the shores
of my native land, and I did not think that she
would now be deceitful or unpropitious, since I
had braved so many dangers in the Southern
Pacific. When the anchor was weighed for our
departure, and our kind friends came to take leave
of me, I thought only of a pleasant sail, as on a
party of pleasure. The countenances of the
hardy seamen, inured to all climates, and at home
in all countries, seemed to me to glow with the
thoughts of their native land, and they sprang to
their duties as if they had turned their faces
homeward.

CHAPTER X.

Conchology—The Pearl-oyster—The Nautilus—The large Shell
used for War Trumpets—The Eyestone—Character of Sailors
—Causes of their Ignorance—Their Errors on the Side of Virtue—The Neglect of their Education—United States' Ship
Vincennes—Manner in which Seamen should be treated—
Character and Description of Sunday and Monday, two Natives brought Home in the Antarctic

On the voyage to New-York from Bordeaux, I
took an opportunity, in pleasant weather, to
arrange the shells I had been collecting in the
Southern Pacific. I was, when quite young, much
pleased with the beauty of shells, and had received
from sea-faring connexions a pretty collection.
This taste I afterward gratified in gathering them
on the beaches of the many islands at which we
made a shorter or longer stay. My passion for
conchology increased when I turned to writings
on the subject, and found how long this branch of
natural history had attracted the attention of mankind, and how much had been done towards classifying and describing the great variety of shells. I
had considered them the mere playthings of taste,
nor once dreamed that such philosophers as those
of Greece had paid attention to picking up and
describing shells : but I was happy to find that
those things which gave me so much pleasure
were really among matters of importance. More
than two thousand years ago Aristotle made a
treatise upon conchology for the benefit of his pupil

Alexander the Great. At first it seemed strange
to me that he who was deep in the mysteries of
logic could stoop to examine the shell of a muscle,
or that he who was grasping at universal empire
could listen to a discourse on shells ; but I believe
the more intelligent the age and nation are, the
more these minute subjects are attended to, for
during all the night of darkness when the world
was overrun with superstition, no attention was
paid to natural history. Those who were discuss-
ing absurd questions in theology were likely to
neglect the works of God as displayed in his creation and providence.   A little more than half a
century since, the science of conchology was re-
vived and enlarged, and is now in a train to
become extensively understood.   The admirable
construction of shells for the purposes for which
they were intended, and the beautifully variegated
colours with which many of them are adorned,
afford additional proof to the observer of nature
of the superintending hand of Providence extended even to the minutest objects of creation.
It is a beautiful sight to look along the shores
of some of the islands near the equator and
mark the endless variety of shells thrown up by
the winds and waves—the houses of tenants long
since dead ; but if we could rake the bottom of
the sea near those islands and find the living
shells, they would be much more beautiful.
The shells the divers brought us with the inhabitant alive were in beauty of tints far more
exquisite than those bleached by the sun and
rains, and washed by ten thousand tides.
The pearl-oyster, as the conch is called, which
contains the pearl, is worthy of examination,

This oyster is about three or four times as large as the common oyster, and, as far as I could learn, a being of higher faculties; he has the power of locomotion, and moves, if at no great distance, or with any considerable speed, backward and forward to find his food. The shell is sometimes called mother-of-pearl ; an expressive term, even if no pearls are found within the shell. The pearl was long supposed to be fixed to the shell, to assist in opening it, or for some other purpose,—Heaven only knows what ; the pearl, however, is not found adhering to the shell, but grows under the most fleshy parts of the oyster, or near his head, leaving a mark upon the shell. This creation, like that of the ambergris, has never been satisfactorily accounted for, and perhaps never will be. The great Author of nature intended, no doubt, that the beings he had endowed with reason should have perpetual enigmas to solve, so that they might be satisfied that they could never reach him by attempting to fathom all the secrets of nature; for he knows their ambition and their pride. The natives of the South Sea islands make these shells useful in the formation of instruments, such as hatchets, spears, fish-hooks, and knives ; and, if not equal to iron and steel, they are vastly superior to those which could be made of silver or gold. It is not a little singular to one living constantly on land that the ancients should have attributed to the sea so many of the loveliest of their mythological creations ; Venus rose from the foam of the ocean, and the Tritons sounded their shells at her birth. These fictions were unquestionably of Indian origin, for there the ocean is most lovely, and the shells the most beautiful. The Greeks got their descriptions second-

handed; for the shores of the Mediterranean or
those of the Red Sea produce no specimens of
conchology to be compared with those of the
islands near the equator.

I had read that Cleopatra dissolved a most valuable pearl in vinegar, and drank it. The vinegar must have been stronger than that which
we had, for I tried one of the almost impercepti-
ble pearls, taken by thousands from these oysters,
and could not dissolve it in a whole day. She, I
think, must have mixed a little water with whatever could dissolve a pearl, or have had a royal
stomach indeed. The ancients must have far
exceeded the moderns in knowledge, or the wonders of early history must have been described
with little regard to truth. If Egypt's queen did
not drink the pearl, she taught her subjects how
to find it. After her restoration by Cæsar to the
throne of the Ptolemies, she pursued the commerce of her ancestors, and grew wealthy beyond
all the Eastern monarchs of her age. Antony
bestowed upon her Phenicia, Cyprus, some part
of Arabia, Crete, and other commercial places.
Her reign is a proof of the intimate connexion
of letters with commerce.

It would require a huge volume to give any
satisfactory account of even the small number
of shells we collected, compared with the myriads on the shores of the islands in the Southern
Pacific. The nautilus, of which we gathered a
great variety, is quite a curiosity, and has held a
high rank in conchology for many reasons. It
is a vessel, and some of the ancient poets, and
modern ones too, make it the prototype of vessels and of sailing. The various species of the
genus are found in most warm countries; they

are of all sizes, from that of your thumb-nail to upwards of eighteen inches from stem to stern,—as the sailors speak of them while sailing along. The living and fleshy part of the nautilus does not weigh much more than an ounce, whereas the shell would hold a quart; but this living part has the power of throwing all the water from the shell, and of sailing by projecting a membrane, which the sailors in their significant manner call a stern-sheet. The outside of the shell is white and smooth, and the inside is of a pearly cast. The natives make these their drinking-cups when polished and ornamented for use. These ornaments are often singular; I have several of them bearing fancy sketches decidedly superior to such as often appear in Ackerman's Repository, for ladies' ornamental work, and the La Belle Assemblée, as patterns for the working of fashionable handkerchiefs or vandikes. And I believe some of the queens and princesses of these isles can arrange and wear a tuft of feathers quite as tastefully as any lady at Almack's at a fashionable ball. These shells are not used for any purpose that I know of among us, but they are certainly as handsome as any large shells we have in our cabinets.

The large shell generally called by the common name of conch is found in these islands in great abundance. These shells are artificially perforated near the top, and are used as the war-trumpet by the natives. They never sound it except as a general signal for muster. The power of it is vastly greater than that of the trumpet, and may be heard farther than any martial instrument in use among civilized men. There is something extremely natural in all the seemingly monstrous fables of the ancients; they made the Triton blow this shell as trumpeter to Neptune, even as far back as Deucalion's flood; and at the sound the waters retired. The sound of this shell can be heard for many miles when blown by a strong-breathed sailor in the mood of amusing himself, without having any classical images in his head. The conch was brought to some parts of our country very early; in fact, I have been informed that some of the original settlers introduced them when they first came here, and used them to call the distant workmen to their meals. History informs us that the Indians in the wars of King Philip were at one time frightened from their purpose by some accidental sound of the dinner-summoning conch; and at a much later period, it was used in the interior of our country to call the inmates of a college to dinner or to prayers. The ancients considered these shells as carrying within them a spirit of echo, and whoever puts one of them to his ear will discover from whence that impression arose. There is a sound of distant waters in his ear; the lashing of the billows upon the beach. What close observers must have been these poetical examiners of nature; and we might add, how many of these impressions remain on the minds of the present generation. Perhaps many of our commonly received notions would not stand the test of modern criticism in an age when nature is so severely scrutinized by philosophers.

There is another little shell, commonly called the eyestone, of which I have seen no satisfactory account, though I do not mean to insinuate that there is none extant. I do not know the classical term for it, and therefore must speak of it by its popular name. The former impression that we had upon this subject was, that the eyestone was gifted with life, which slept in quiet until man wanted its services, when by plunging it into vinegar it was revivified and ready for use. When by some misfortune a moat gets into our eye, the sleeping agent is roused to fitness for use by a powerful acid. That the eyestone discovered such signs of life as to make it susceptible of motion in this acid no one will have the hardihood to deny, for most have seen and can bear testimony to it; and how natural the idea that vitality is connected with motion. The science of the present day, however, is not content to receive any thing on trust; and the notion of the vitality of the eyestone, in common with other popular errors, is now exploded. A few lessons from our old friend Dr. Griscom, I think, would enable any one to conjecture that this stone is an alkali, and the acid being poured upon it gives it action and effervescence, which accounts for its motion round the vessel into which it is placed with the vinegar. Put into the eye, it moves around under the lid by the natural action of the parts with which it comes in contact, and being so smooth—for all its excrescences are destroyed by the acid—it gives no pain ; and working under the lid, often pushes before it any speck or moat, and relieves the eye in a short time. While it is in the eye we forbear to rub the lid for fear that the stone will get out of its place ; of course the eye has a rest which in ordinary occasions of its smarting we should not be disposed to grant it.

I

Many of the phenomena of nature were known to the ancients only by their effects, and it was left to modern science to trace their origin to natural causes. The knowledge of the ancients, being confined almost wholly to the priesthood, offered a ready instrument in their hands to govern the minds of men by superstitious terrors. The light of science, however, is no longer confined to the pagan temple or monkish cloister, and gradually developes in their natural forms many things which superstition and ignorance could only attribute to the supernatural.

I have been astonished that an attempt to reform seamen should have been left to so late a period as it has been. A current opinion has been afloat ever since commerce was introduced into the world, that those who went down to the sea in ships should be rough, bold, and uncivil; and it has been left for moderns to discover that these characteristics are not necessary to make a good sailor. That they should be bold and fearless necessarily arises from their duties, their exposures, and their vicissitudes; cowardice in them would lead to destruction, and they know it. Habit makes them often do an act the consequences of which they do not stop to calculate; they are hardy, generally, from exercise and sea air, enjoy health and strength, and seldom grow indolent from indulging in too much sleep. Profanity is with them rather a degrading habit than a blasphemous feeling or disposition; the officers too often indulge in the vice, and the sailors imitate them. They are superstitious because they are ignorant; constantly seeing remarkable things without being able, by any knowledge they have, of accounting for them, they have recourse to their imaginations for causes, and this power of their minds is without cultivation or taste, and the greater the mystery the better ; but still their hearts seem to be right.

Nineteen-twentieths of the sailors who double the Cape of Good Hope and go into the Eastern seas believe in the truth of the Flying Dutchman ; they have well-authenticated stories of honest seamen, who bore honest testimony to the fact ; and if it was the only way to establish the truth of a matter by the solemn testimony of witnesses, this would be as well supported as any event in history. Cotton Mather speaks of a phantom-ship which appeared near the harbour of Boston. A vessel had long been missing, and the friends of those on board her became distressed; prayers were offered up for their safety, but when she was quite given over, a ship was distinctly seen by the people of Boston coming in under full sail. So distinctly was she seen, that men were visible on her decks ; she came on swimmingly for an hour or two, when in an instant she vanished, and was never heard of or seen any more. It was considered by that pious and learned man, and of course by most others, that this was a kind vision from the Almighty to assure all those interested in the fate of the ship that she was lost, and all hands perished. Those who did not believe in this interference of Providence to shadow out such an event, did not know how to account for the phenomenon, and of course were silent upon it. For nearly two centuries this story was told, to the belief of many, and to the amusement of others, when an explanation was given by a similar appearance in the city of New-York. In the fall of 1826, the appearance of

several vessels was seen from the Battery upon
the horizon, clearly and distinctly, when the ships
whose images were reflected were not within
sight. These images, by refraction, were thrown
on a cloud beyond them by the rays of the sun;
and while many wondered the philosophers explained, and a satisfactory solution of Cotton
Mather's story was made out. Some ship from
the north was sailing towards the south, and not
wishing to enter the port of Boston, was so situated as to be reflected on such a cloud; and hence
arose the appearance which was proved beyond
a doubt, yet was not believed by the reasoning
people of subsequent times.

There can be no doubt of the fact that in these
seas where the phenomenon of the Flying Dutchman has been again and again seen, that this
effect is reducible to the same cause. The sailors
have a tradition that this Flying Dutchman and
his crew were wicked enough to deny the Christian religion, and to trample the cross under their
feet for gain, with imprecations upon their heads
if they did not despise it; such as a wish that
if they were not sincere in their renunciation,
they might never return again to their native
land. For this unpardonable sin, this vessel
and its crew were doomed to fly from place
to place until the world should be destroyed.
This very prejudice, however, was on the side
of virtue, and has been made use of to keep seamen from denying their faith, even in the midst
of their blasphemy; and although it is known
that the Mohammedans make strenuous efforts
to induce a Christian to profess their faith, yet
but few even of the most profligate of the sailors
of Christian nations have been known to change

their religion, even when the temptations held out were of the most captivating kind.

The sailor is generous, bold, and faithful, with even prejudices that are on the side of virtue; why, then, is he left in ignorance, and hardly reckoned a part of the intellectual or moral world? It has not been his fault half so much as the fault of those who had the control of him. Those who employed him, and could not do without his services, reasoned like the despot :— " My authority is at an end when they know any thing more than mere seamanship; if they could navigate as well as I can, they would take my ship and go where they please with her." This reasoning might be true if they were to be instructed in science without any attention to morals. This subject has now become of importance to our country, considering the great number of sailors we have. Taking the navy, and those engaged in foreign and domestic commerce and the fisheries, there cannot be less than sixty thousand; forty-three thousand of these are employed in commerce, and ten thousand in the navy. Instruction might be given to all these at an easy and cheap rate, and they might be made more respectable citizens without injuring them as sailors. Merchants often say, if you enlighten these men, who are now only so many good machines to work or fight a ship, and make them understand their situation, you raise at once the price of wages, and commerce will not afford this. But can they not at the same time see that this could not be an evil of long continuance, for the wages are always incorporated with other expenses on a cargo, and the consumer, not the merchant, pays for it. But is the objection true? Would not the

regularity of the conduct of seamen lessen en-
surance, and produce more despatch in voyages,
and by these means make a balance in favour of
the merchant in the end ? If sailors were properly educated and kept sober, there would be less
chance of their turning pirates, and of commit-
ting crimes at which all mankind shudder; and
which are now becoming so prevalent that
scarcely a paper is issued without some mention
of the loss of lives and property by piracy.
Humanity is appalled at some of these atrocities;
the naval force is called upon to avenge the in-
juries: but this moral discipline would do better,—
it would, in most instances, prevent them.

It is not a little extraordinary that all nations
should so far forget themselves as to have no
system of instruction or discipline for sailors, except such as is left by law in the discretion of
masters of vessels. There is in the world at
least a million of seamen, who are engaged in
fighting their country's battles, or assisting in the
sailing of vessels of merchandise, or in the several fisheries, and hardly a school among them
all. No farmer hires a man who is not recom-
mended to him as an able-bodied man, and one
well acquainted with his duties; yet a merchant
waits, after he has fixed upon his voyage, selected
his master, and got his vessel loaded and just fit
for sea, and then drums up his crew on short
notice, only inquiring if they be good seamen,
without thinking of their moral characters at all,
or making the slightest inquiry whether the man
they ship is a pirate or an honest seaman. As
long as this is the case, and there are so many
bad men who resort to the seas, perhaps to escape
the punishment due to their crimes, no wonder that

so many deeds of horror are perpetrated. Inquiry should be made into every man's character before he ships, and then proper arrangements made to treat him well on the voyage as to food and instruction. I believe this good work has been begun in many of the seaport towns in this country. Provision has been made for mariners' churches, and with no doubt some fanaticism, much good has been done in many respects. In the navy there are now some chaplains who can both preach and pray. I would not have a ship a conventicle; but much may be done without any cant or overstrained piety. Get such men thinking right, and you will soon find them acting well. Thus educated, instead of sowing the seeds of profligacy wherever they went, we should find them seeking to do good ; and opportunities often occurring, much might be effected by them in all parts of the world. Those with whom these men are connected on shore would be benefited by their example, and they would not only do good abroad, but in time the wave of their exertions would be *rolled* back to bless the land of their birth and the home of their affections. Educate sailors, and they would contract binding ties, which is not often the case now. We are, and ever shall be, a great commercial people ; of course a navy will be constantly kept up ; and is it not of vital importance that we should set about a school for reform ?

Just before we arrived at Manilla, the United States' sloop-of-war Vincennes visited the place. She was, in all respects, a fine ship ; the people of Manilla spoke of her neatness, her order, and the decorum of her crew. There was no revelling in her, nor by her crew out of her ; the control over

them was perfect. This was owing to the honourable agreement between the captain and the chap-
lain; they understood each other, and the crew
understood both. All things were put in order
by concert at head-quarters, and of course carried
into effect; both officers were men of sense, and
expected no more than could be performed by
men; but they took every efficient measure to
bring the minds of the crew to a just sense of
reasoning; and instruction was going on while
duty was performed. This was as it should be;
and no ship ever yet went round the world with
so much ease, with so little loss of human life,
and with so much harmony, as the Vincennes.
It was only an ordinary voyage to them, but extraordinary, in fact, to every looker-on. The discipline of the crew was a source of wonder to the
people of every place they visited. This is only a
sample of what may be done: the allowance of
whiskey should be cut off by fair contract, and
something substituted in its place. Government
should not save by any of these regulations, but
should rather over than under-pay; let good and
wholesome meals be always provided, and good
and wholesome instruction be constantly going
on, and the seamen would be content, and the ship
for ever secure. It has always been found that
the true Christian will fight like a lion; it has
never been found that principle has destroyed
mental energy, but, on the contrary, has sustained
it through every contest. Change the moral
character of your seamen, and you make them
invincible; let the modes of instruction be simple
and easy, not made as a task, but granted as a
boon, and all will be right. It is my belief that
a crew of men formed on these principles, and so

trained and treated, would not flinch from twice
their number of such as are commonly found in
what has been emphatically called "the floating
hells of the sea." I am not one of those fanatics
who think that all the world are to be made Christians and devotees at once, and that all duty is to
be absorbed in the forms of religion. No; but
from what I have seen, I believe that every ship's
crew can be made a well-regulated family, in
which decency and decorum may be found as
well as on shore. That vice can be rooted out of
the world entirely I am not so weak as to suppose; but I do believe that where law is so supported by principle, sailors can be made as good
men as others, and governed as easily. If there
was ever any meaning in the oft-repeated declaration of the good Bishop of Cloyne, that

"Westward the star of empire takes its way,"

it was to rise in some moral, not natural relation.
If man is here to rise to higher eminence as an
intelligent being than he ever did in the old
world, it is not from his capability of destroying,
but from a disposition to benefit his species,—
still to protect himself. Man is mentally and
corporally enfeebled by vice, and his energies
and exploits are immediately connected with his
health and his sanity of mind. The phrensy of
inebriation may last for a few moments, but the
calm determination of honest feelings and clear
views is worth much more than all the fury of
accidental excitement. I know that there are
honest men who think these reasonings a
species of fanaticism, and I do not doubt that
some things said at the Bethels and mariners'

I 3

churches may savour of fanaticism; but that is
no argument against the attempts to make sailors
rational, and moral, and religious beings; it
never was, and never will be the case, that a reform was conducted in all respects by the cool
dictates of the understanding.

I would commence systematically. In the
first place, I would introduce a few well-written
epitomes of moral and religious duties, with
some interesting anecdotes of Christian mariners.
They should be without sectarianism, or any
thing that had a bearing that way; and, in addi-
tion, a fair epitome of the best voyages now extant should be made up for the use of the crew.
Every thing should be fairly used to make the
profession appear in its true and honourable light,
without colouring or deceit; every sailor should
learn, as by this mirror, to see and respect himself. By small treatises, he should be taught his
duties in every way. If his duties as a seaman
were clearly laid down, he would learn them in
half the time he now does by curses and flog-
gings. He should then be carried to higher
views of science and navigation, and should consider himself an intelligent being, engaged in an
honest cause, and for a proper end. This may
seem chimerical to one who has several ships,
and wishes to get them navigated as cheap as
possible; but the calculations and arguments
of any one should yield to general interest and
common understanding. When there were but
three or four banks in the United States, the
stockholders, it is said, objected to having any
more, as the mysteries of managing them were
above the ordinary comprehension. The mystery of managing the moral and temporal con-

dition of sailors may be thought to be above the comprehension of a woman; but, however, one thing is certain, that if my remarks are of no service, they are at least harmless. To ship a sailor, learn him to do his duty, and to bring him back safe after he has honestly and honourably discharged his duty, has no mystery in it, but a good deal of common sense.

Our manufacturing establishments, it is said, will be exempt from many of the evils which are found in those of Europe, because in most of them provision is made that the young of both sexes shall not grow up in ignorance; and why should not this principle be incorporated into our commercial establishments? Merchants have made and are making ample provision to preserve the morals and to enlighten the minds of their clerks, to prevent fraud and peculation; and why should not equal attention be paid to the moral and intellectual improvement of mariners? To them, in fact, as much is intrusted, without the same ready means to bring them to a sense of justice. Provision should be made to instruct sailors when out of employment. A plan has lately been suggested by a patriotic and intelligent member of Congress to make the whole army of the United States one great seminary of instruction, and to dismiss all its idle and good-for-nothing drones, and introduce youthful ambition in their place. The plan, I verily believe, will succeed when it is properly understood, the army will be made much more efficient than it now is, and thousands of good citizens will be added to the republic. If the contemplated improvements in the condition of soldiers cannot all be realized with respect to seamen, still an approximation can be made, and the sailor, should he be disabled or disinclined to follow his profession, may be enabled to fill some station in society for which he is fitted : but according to the present system, when a sailor can no longer discharge his duties on ship-board, he is considered as an outcast from society, and must expire in some asylum of charity, or die by excited intemperance. This is wrong ; the moralists and philanthropists of the age should set about devising some remedy for these evils, and the sooner they engage in it the better.

I had almost forgotten to state that while visiting those islands near the equator where we had some skirmishes with the natives, we took a prisoner, whom, from the day on which he was taken, we called MONDAY. He was picked up from the water : the canoe in which he was being destroyed by the cannon-shot, he took to the water, and being wounded, was taken in by our boat's crew sent for that purpose. He is apparently about twenty-two years of age, five feet eight inches high, stout made, and quick in his movements. He is rather sullen in his temper, but has never appeared vindictive to us. He is ingenious, and very imitative. At first he seemed to wish to remain in ignorance, but after a while came to a better disposition, and was desirous, in some measure, to oblige. His countenance is that of a savage in every respect ; he has the Indian high cheek-bones and the dark humours of the eye. He is not of a strong constitution, seeming rather inclined to consumption ; but how any being could have that complaint who was born and lived in the climate he did I cannot tell. Perhaps the thoughts of being a prisoner preyed on his mind, and the sickness of his heart was taken for that of another kind. At times this savage would sit and look steadfastly upon the ocean towards, as he probably thought, the point from whence he came, for whole hours together. Every kindness was shown him ; he ate what he pleased, and when, and not a blow was ever given him by any one ; the sailors having strict orders not to disturb him nor his companion. He wandered about the deck, and showed at length some marks of interest in things around him. He soon became familiar to clothes, and fond of them.

SUNDAY was a native of more importance; from another island, taken shortly before Monday. He is a stout, well-made man, of five feet eleven inches in height, weighs about two hundred pounds, and is remarkably strong and active. He is without doubt a chief among his tribe, for he led the attack upon us, and bore himself bravely. His corporeal strength is wonderful ; no one on board our vessel possessed equal muscular power. He is supposed to be about thirty-five years of age, and is very tractable. He soon learned many English words, and seemed anxious to know as much as he could. He is very good-natured, docile, and obliging ; and understands sufficient of our language to know that he has a promise from my husband that he shall return to his native land as soon as circumstances will permit. He has more of the African cast of features than the inhabitants of most of the islands we visited. He states that he had three wives, to which number his rank entitled him, being the son of the king of the group, who was an old man, and did not come out to battle. This is probable, for we never perceived the slightest disposition in him

to utter a falsehood. He seems to be open, generous, and willing to do any thing he can for others;
he is extremely anxious to return to his native
island, and promises to make them all do right.

I am far from the opinion that these people
whom we call savages have the worst dispositions of any people on earth ; on the contrary, I
believe that if their hearts could first be reached by
kindness, they could easily be brought to observe
the rules and decencies of society. I state this for
the encouragement of those who may hereafter become missionaries to these benighted parts of the
earth. This very savage may, and I trust will,
be an efficient instrument in opening a way for
the labours of pious men who may be sent into
these regions. Besides the good it will do, will
it not be a source of happiness to those engaged
in such a cause ? Is there not a disposition in
every enterprising mind to erect some memorial
of his exertions which will endure beyond the
time he may live ? Do not these almost unknown
regions afford an opportunity for virtuous distinction ? To carry civilization and Christianity to
such remote parts of the earth would have given
joy to the apostles themselves ; and is it not a
happy reflection to the zealous good man, that
there is still a wide field for him and his successors?
I never saw happier beings than the missionaries
in the island of New-Zealand, although so far
from friends and country, and the good of savage
men their only reward. I have often thought of
the sincerity of these people, who were not among
the poor and destitute in their own country, but
possessed of means to live and bear a respectable
part in society. They labour from one year to another, with all the care of those who have the cure

of souls, in truth and reality thinking of no recompense this side of heaven. How sincere the religion—how warm the faith, that can support them in all this! It is almost equal to that expressed by St. Paul, who could wish himself condemned for Christ's sake. The spirit and zeal of him of Tarsus is abroad, united with something of the sweet affections of him whom Christ loved ; at least I thought so when I visited New-Zealand. I loved them for staying there, but I should not have dared to ask my heart if I could join them ; I should have feared a worldly answer from myself, but, thank Heaven, I can never be put to the test.

CHAPTER XI.

Observations on the Progress of Discovery—Remarks on the
Marine of various Nations—Aurora Borealis—Anecdote of its
Appearance early in the last Century.

THE glories of discovery are divided among
the maritime nations of Europe with our own
country. Those that were once famous on
the ocean are not so now. Those who sailed
from the Gulf of Finland, and spread terror
through Europe, are not now known as having
any navy, or vessels of commerce. The Portuguese are seldom found at this day in their
own discovered countries ; and the Spaniards
are hardly known in the countries over which
the nation still holds sway. I do not know
that either of these nations have, for many years,
had a ship of discovery on the seas, on which
they once were the masters and lords of every
wave, and but very few pursuing the regular
course of commerce. To a Spaniard who calls
to mind the rank which his country once held
among the nations, when the Indies and the
greater part of Europe acknowledged her su-
premacy, it must be a melancholy reflection,
that empire has passed or is passing away from
her. The galleons which once sailed from Manilla to South America, and to Spain, are now
only reminiscences of history ; no such thing is
seen in these seas, and it requires some degree
of faith to believe they ever existed. If the

Spanish ships are scarce, the Portuguese are scarcer; a vessel may sail the globe without meeting one of either nation. The Prussians and Austrians never put in any claim for the honour of discovery: and Denmark and Sweden can boast of but little more for these three centuries past. Venice, and Genoa, and Florence are now as if they had never been, in a commercial point of view. Most of the nations who once contended for fame as discoverers, do so no more. The only flags now to be met with are those of England, France, Russia, the United States, and now and then one of the kingdom of the Netherlands. The commerce of Holland is reviving— she has long been in the background, but is certainly rising in enterprise and power. The autocrat of all the Russias has evinced a desire that his empire should be ranked among the commercial and naval nations of the world, and has been at some expense to support this assumption. If his share in the bloody battle of Navarino has done him no honour, the voyage of Von Kotzebue has. Russia has too deep an interest in the Western Pacific not to have a respectable force on the North-west Coast. Russia is slowly, but surely, extending her commerce and maritime power over every sea, and will make her way if she pursues her present policy. France has not extended her empire much since the battles of the Nile and Trafalgar, but is increasing her marine with no humble objects in view. Her navy now falls but little short in point of numbers to that of Great Britain, and her colonies are next to the British in fertility and commerce. France has always in modern times, of which we are speaking, been ambitious to have

her share in exploring and in governing the world.
She may be said to watch every point of inspection along the deep ; but since her disasters in the
great battles with England, with less than her
former display, yet, I have no doubt, with all her
former sagacity. The discoveries of England
are made public by government at once ; but
the French discoveries are only partially given
to the world ; since the days of La Perouse,
they have not published any thing of consequence. If France is suffered to remain in peace,
we may rely upon it she will have no humble
views of her knowledge and her power. Her ambition was always great, and as she has gained
in intelligence, she has lost nothing of her pride
or her enterprise.

Although there is no parade made about it, we
find French ships everywhere. They pursue
their course in silent duty, but not without gaining information. England, it is true, considers
the ocean as her own, and sails it as if this
superiority was never to be disputed. The imposing appearance of her ships was well calculated to impress the minds of the people in every
distant region they visited with an idea of the
power and importance of the empire, especially
when contrasted with the smaller size and inferior equipment of those of other European nations. The natives possessed no other means of
judging of the relative importance of the countries which traded with them ; and it is to be
presumed that no endeavour was spared by those
who navigated the British vessels to increase
this favourable impression. From this cause
it has arisen that every expression of admiration and reverence that these aborigines have

at command has been exhausted on the British
navy.   This influence is fairly earned, however
inimical it may be to the views of nations at this
day, when all are strenuously contending for
their rights.   I know not how they can remedy
the evil which is experienced by the superiority of
England, except by emulating that country in their
commercial exertions in every part of the world.
The United States, if her commerce and marine
increase as they have done for twenty years past,
will be nearly, in twenty years to come, as much
interested in the trade of the southern hemisphere
as England.   The visits of our vessels of war to the
remote parts of the Western and Eastern Pacific
have had a good effect on the minds of the Indians,
Malays, and Chinese, who think nothing of justice,
but only as it may be enforced by power.   Some
civilized nations must in time be masters of these
remote islands, and it would be well for us to have
a share in the influence that may be exercised in
this new world abounding in articles of commerce.
Settlements on some of the numerous islands
lately discovered by American navigators would
be acceptable to the whaling ships as well as to
other vessels, and would create a new market for
many of our articles of commerce.   The field is as
wide for the philanthropist as for the merchant,
and he would be as eager to occupy it.

The maritime power of Russia is one of those
that will increase, if not rapidly, yet surely.   The
spirit of Peter the Great is in existence in that
government, and will not easily be driven out of
it ; he said, in the pride of valour, " Nature has
but one Russia, and it shall have no rival."
At that time he hardly knew that an empire
had been planted in this western world, which

now bids fair to share the honours of national
influence with Russia. The opening of the Eux-
ine will give Russia facilities for commerce and for
increasing her navy, which she has never before
possessed, and there can be no question but that
she will avail herself of every advantage she
gains.

The naval character of the people of the United
States may be said almost to be incorporated with,
and form a part of their nature. Our forefathers
began to navigate the ocean almost as soon as they
had landed on these shores : more than a hundred years since, the colonies had a spirited little
navy, that carried the provisions and troops in
1717 to Canada. In the war of 1745 the naval
power of the country was respectable if not formidable. Vessels of considerable size were sent by
the colonies to the siege of Louisburg. In the war
of 1755, and onward to 1763, American sailors
were distinguished for enterprise and bravery. In
that of 1775 the colonies astonished the English by
the number and spirit of their private armed vessels,
and the Congress in 1776 created a considerable
marine, which was on the ocean in a very short
time. The national and private armed ships, if
our histories of that age be correct, took from the
enemy fifteen hundred vessels. The history of
that proud age has not as yet been fully written ;
there are many heroes as yet to be celebrated by
our biographers. I may be thought enthusiastic
in all this, but the achievements of those who
won for us the high station and proud name
we boast, I confess, have taken deep hold of
my mind, and I will make no more apology
for talking about them. In 1798 the nation was
awakened by the insult offered our flag by France ;

and a navy, a small, but spirited one, was instantly built, and commissioned to defend our commerce. Now it was that our country began to count the cost and realize the value of a navy. The orders under which our fleet sailed at first were so restricted, that not much was done excepting by way of protection; but when these orders were enlarged they captured many vessels, nearly a hundred, and recaptured many which the French cruisers had taken from the citizens of the United States. In this short war there were some fine specimens of naval character developed by our gallant officers. Captains Truxton, Little, and Shaw, and others, gained an imperishable name by their bravery and skill. Our people had hoped that the little navy would be cherished; but the policy of that day was against it, and all our ships were sold but a few frigates. This sacrifice in the end was of no importance, although a subject of great mortification to the merchants and the friends of the navy; but the glory it had won was secured, whatever became of the vessels. We had satisfied ourselves that man had not degenerated in our country, that his muscle and nerve were as good as those of any other nation. The parsimonious were satisfied that we could build and maintain a navy at as little cost as any other nation; and the timid began to think that we could fight in a good cause. Still our mother country regarded our power on the ocean as insignificant. They had fought France so easily, that they thought no honour was acquired by contending with them on equal terms. The fates were determined we should have no chance to grow rusty in our naval experience. All the piratical powers, whose rob-

beries and extortions had been borne so long by the
nations of Europe, expected that the commerce
of the new and feeble nation, as they thought us,
would become an easy prey. The state of the times
made it necessary for us, as a nation, to tamely
purchase peace and immunity from Morocco and
Algiers. This was galling to a free people, but
policy required that we should suffer in silence;
still we were not prepared to bear the yoke for ever.
In 1800 the ship commissioned to carry tribute
to the Dey of Algiers was sent by this savage
on a mission to his master, the Grand Seignor at
Constantinople. This indignity was submitted
to in order to exempt our mariners from being
taken as slaves, and suffering indignities worse
than death. These pirates had long been the
scourge of nations; for a thousand years they
had held a piratical sway from the pillars of Her-
cules all along the shores of the Mediterranean.
To their everlasting disgrace, Spain, Portugal,
France, and England, with Denmark and Sweden, paid them tribute. At times some of the
Christian nations had attempted to subdue these
hordes of barbarians, and made great efforts for
the purpose, but without success. In 1800, when
the Bashaw of Tripoli demanded tribute of us in
the most insulting manner, the people of the
United States called aloud to have these freebooters and assassins punished. The Bey of Tunis
raised his voice for tribute, and with the full
belief that his exactions would be complied with.
The Bashaw of Tripoli declared war with the
United States, thinking to strike terror into the
New World. Soon after this declaration of war,
one of our oldest naval commanders was sent
out with a squadron of observation, consisting of

three frigates and a schooner. His instructions
were full of caution, he was not to fight if he
could help it ; but this could not be avoided. On
the 6th of August, 1801, Lieutenant Stewart in
the Enterprise, of only 12 guns, took a Tripolitan
ship of war, the first that ever was subdued by
our prowess. The barbarian had more guns than
the Enterprise. She had twenty killed, and
thirty wounded in the action ; but there was not
one American injured. Our naval tactics were
now acknowledged to be of the first order.

In the spring of 1802 a squadron was sent out
under the command of Captain R. V. Morris, who,
being charged with want of energy, was superseded by Preble. It is said, however, that Morris
showed no want of courage, but acted, as he
thought, according to his instructions. Never
was there a better commander than Preble. He
was accompanied by Bainbridge, Decatur, Charles
Morris, MacDonough, and others, since been
made conspicuous by their deeds. The squadron blockaded Tripoli, and watched the movements of Algiers, Morocco, and Tunis, which,
like tigers, were ready to start from their repose on their prey. The emperor of Morocco
came to terms, and the Dey of Algiers was quiet,
when Preble determined to chastise Tripoli with
the force he had with him, consisting of a few
Neapolitan gun-boats, which were but little better
than so many mud-scows. On the 3d of August, 1804, the American commander made the
first attack. This was appalling to the barbarian, and he lessened his demands of tribute and
ransom ; but his terms were not admissible, and
another attack was made on the 5th. On the
28th, Commodore Preble attacked them again, as

also on the 3d of September. Preble was now superseded, and left the Mediterranean. Peace was concluded the next summer between Tripoli and the United States on equitable terms.

This event astounded all Europe ; that a new power, of no note or name, should have carried on a war with such slight means, and to so glorious a termination, was indeed surprising. The nations of Europe could hardly be convinced of the fact that the thing should have been attempted, but to find it achieved surpassed all wonder. His holiness believed it a miracle in favour of the Christian church, and said almost as much in his communications upon the subject; and it was indeed bordering on the miraculous, that a few ships of an infant country should instantly effect what powerful nations had attempted unsuccessfully for ages. The story was carried even to the harem of the sultan, and he stared at the account of our prowess. The wretches released from slavery sent the cry of joy abroad, and it was echoed by their friends throughout the world. Venice, Genoa, Naples, Portugal, Spain, and other powers had been foiled in their attempts on the smallest of these Barbary powers ; but we had taught them civilization in a short time. The corsair who formerly had sailed with the utmost insolence in these seas now fled from the first appearance of an American sloop-of-war, as if it were a vessel of the largest class. Their modes of warfare had been considered as most terrible ; but Preble taught the world that they were not ᵒ formidable, and might be attacked by any enterprising foe. This war was one which not only showed the falsity of the general estimate of barbarian power, but also of the power of civilized nations in comparison with them. These pirates were more terrific than powerful.

From this war to that of 1812, our navy was not much increased, nor extensively employed. Many were apprehensive that its character would be lost in peace; and already many statesmen began to think that the United States could do without a navy. The officers of the navy knew that they had to fight themselves into fame, and to conquer the prejudices of the world.

A new field of glory offered itself to our brave mariners, in the war of 1812 ; and by them it was most nobly improved. Hull opened the scene with great gallantry and success ; he was followed up by Jones, Lawrence, Perry, Chauncey, Stewart, Decatur, Blakeley, and by so many others who won fame by bravery and intelligence, that it is almost invidious to mention names. These brave men have already been honoured by the American people, and will be mentioned in history ; and their fame will help to increase the public favour towards a navy. It is said that we have fifty vessels of war, nearly half of which are in commission. The whole are supported by less than three millions of dollars annually : so that for this proud defence the population is not taxed to the amount of twenty-five cents a head yearly. The French, which is supported at less cost than any other European navy, requires an expenditure four times as great as ours, and the British nine times as much. To keep the peace of the world at the present time, there are about 550 vessels of war in commission. Our force in the different seas is about a twentieth part of this power, and yet we have a much larger proportion of the commerce.

K

of the world to protect than this amounts to. But why all these calculations? say my fair readers. I answer, that I have been for nearly two years almost constantly on the high seas, have reflected much upon this subject, and have some confidence in my own view of it.

It is pleasant to pass from these calculations to contemplate the phenomena of nature, which are for ever giving us variety and food for thought. One evening, on my homeward voyage, I was called by my brother, who was devoted to my happiness, to witness a brilliant aurora borealis. I had hoped in the southern latitudes to have seen an aurora australis; but perhaps we had not sailed sufficiently south for a fair sight of this phenomenon; but a northern light was now illumining the heavens. It was not a novelty, for I had been often called by my friends to observe its occurrence while a schoolgirl; but it now appeared to me as something strange, probably because I had a better habit of observation. The sun had been down about an hour, when a dark cloud fringed the horizon, two or three degrees above it: this cloud was edged with white, sometimes changing to a brilliant fire colour: then arrows of light would dart from the cloud, and stream high in the heavens. Then the clouds would be seen above the light, and new lights would rise on the second band of darkness, converging to a point almost over our heads. The shapes of light were constantly changing: now resembling a volcano, and then pyramids, or burning cities, as the imagination fixed a resemblance on the forms of the instant, and it was only an instant that they remained the same. Sometimes the

fire would be seen streaming up on the left, and
sometimes on the right. The sun, moon, volcanoes, electricity, and other causes, are said to
produce this illumination of the heavens; whether it is caused by one or all I know not, and
perhaps it is not of any great importance to know,
only as a gratification to the inquiring mind.
This phenomenon was first seen in North America in 1719, on the 17th of December; but the
causes which produced it then and now must have
existed from the creation of the world; and it is
strange that it should not have been recorded in the
annals of the New World before. The historian
of the Jews makes mention of appearances which
the men of those days considered as supernatural,
such as armies fighting in the air, and pouring
squadron upon squadron, until the heavens were
one entire battle-field. These omens portended,
as they thought, the destruction of the favoured
city of the Most High. It is not surprising that
before the progress of modern science such events
should produce such impressions. It is the glory
of the present age, that we have the opportunity
of tracing many things to their causes, and at the
same time reverence the Creator of them as much
as those of former days.

A good story is told of the influence of the
aurora borealis on the minds of some unacquainted with its natural causes in the early part of the
last century, in our country. A marriage had
been agreed upon between the son of a merchant
and the daughter of a highly respectable land-
holder. The first day of the year was named as
the happy one. The company, as it was usual
in those days to invite all the connexions and
relations, however remote, was very numerous,

and in great glee; the sun set, and a most beautiful aurora borealis appeared ; the streams of fire
were thrown nearly to the zenith ; all eyes were
upon it, viewing the scene without fear, for they
had heard that it passed away harmlessly when
it appeared before. The good father of the young
lady seemed distressed, and in the most solemn
manner announced his determination to put off
the wedding for that evening. This threw the
whole company into consternation. The young
couple looked disappointed, but said nothing, for
that was a period of parental severity. At length,
the clergyman arrived : he had been delayed by
making some notes upon the phenomenon then
before their eyes. The determination of the old
gentleman was communicated to him privately,
of which he seemed to take no notice, but
went on explaining to all present as much as
was then known by philosophers on the subject, and perhaps they knew about as much
then as they now do. He expatiated upon the
benevolence of the Deity, and suggested that this
was probably one way which he had ordered to
keep the atmosphere in the frozen regions in a
proper state for respiration by the inhabitants,
who were now without a cheering ray of the
blessed sun ; that many months would pass
away before the luminary would rise upon them ;
and that the electricity agitated in this manner
was as harmless as heat-lightning, and assisted
the poor Laplanders and other nations to procure
their food. He went on to illustrate his position
by showing that the eclipses of the sun and
moon, which were once supposed to portend disasters, were now used by the astronomer to
measure time with accuracy, and to correct the

chronology of past ages; and, in fine, to support the truths of the great volume of inspiration. The old man listened to all that was said with great attention, and at length came forward and avowed his conviction of his error, in viewing the northern lights as a manifestation of Divine displeasure. The marriage ceremony was performed, and all were happy. How much good a clergyman can do when he unites the wisdom of the serpent with the harmlessness of the dove.

CHAPTER XII.

Reflections on drawing near my Native Land—The Difficulties
Women experience in gaining Information—The Value of
Commerce—The Influence of Women—Love of the Ocean
—Farewell to it—Sensations on arriving in the Harbour of
New-York—Reaching Home—Public Attentions shown to
my Husband and myself—Gratitude to Heaven for a safe
Return.

I now felt that I was drawing near my native
land, and began to question myself as to what
purpose I had spent my time during this long
and to me interesting voyage. Had I treasured
up all the knowledge that I might have done?
was a natural question. It is hard to satisfy
one's self upon such an inquiry; but I had done
something towards it. I was not prepared by
education or habits to make the most of my situation, but still the consoling reflection arose that
I had never distrusted Providence; had never
repined; and, as far as I was able, cheered my husband in all his misfortunes—and they were not a
few. I felt myself a much graver matron than
when I embarked, and had more settled and, as I
thought, more rational opinions for the government of life. I had suffered much, but enjoyed
more; I had laid up a stock to reflect and reason
upon during my future days; I had left my child,
a short time to him, a long one indeed to me, but
I thought I had learned enough to balance the
pain of this absence in the attainment of that dis-

cretion which a mother should have in bringing
up a child. It is by the kindness of Heaven that
mothers do as well as they are found to do; for
most of them in the early part of their days can
have only the philosophy of the heart to direct
them, not that of the head. My adventurous
course was not a source of pride to me,—it was
not for any specific purpose that I became a voyager, but simply to be a companion of my husband : my feelings or reasonings were uncon-
trolled, and the views I have taken of things, if
not deep, are just as an unlearned mind would
see them. Every thing was rare and strange to
me, and necessarily excited my curiosity. If I
had ever contemplated taking such a voyage, I
think I should have been better prepared to bring
home something more worthy of myself and my
countrywomen ; but as it is, they must take my
intention for my deeds. The great difficulty we
women feel in collecting information, is the want
of order and classification of our thoughts ; and
we therefore labour much harder to arrive at true
conclusions than those who have a regular
pigeon-hole in which to place all sorts of information. Perhaps those who cabinet whatever they
think worth preserving, do not enjoy them so
much as we who think only of amusing ourselves,
without enlightening others. I doubt whether a
scientific observer would have had more thoughts
than passed through my teeming brain ; but he
would have known how to arrange them, and
have drawn conclusions tending to establish
known truths, or elicit new ones ; while whatever observations or conclusions I might make
were liable to be dispersed for not knowing where
to preserve them. The unstudied and unprac-

tised mind, however, observes many things that
might escape the notice of the best educated.

Every vessel we met I amused myself with
considering as a messenger to bring us some
tidings from the friends we left at our departure;
but they often passed us at too great a distance to
speak to them, and as it was a time of peace and
the weather fair, we left each other with a plea-
surable sensation, certain that each was well provided with necessaries for the remainder of the
voyage.   These sights thickened as we came
nearer our own shores, and afforded new proofs
that commercial enterprise was the characteristic
of our countrymen.

On arriving so near the termination of my
voyage, and taking a retrospective view of what
had principally fixed my attention during its continuance, I felt my mind drawn to the contemplation of the regions we had visited in the Southern Pacific.   I hope to live to see the islands in
this ocean inhabited by my countrymen, under
the protection of my country.   There is no ob-
stacle in the way of this.   That the Kings of
Portugal or Spain first erected their standard in
those seas is nothing, or that the pope issued his
bull in their favour is now nothing; but that
they who discover should possess, if they choose,
is the common sense law of nations.   Settlements
might be made on some of the islands we have
discovered, with every prospect of securing the
commerce of those seas, or at least with sharing
it with other nations.   We have existed at all
only about two centuries, and as an independent
and free nation, acknowledged and received into
the great family about half a century; and yet we
are considered the third commercial people on the

globe. We were prosperous as carriers of the commodities of other nations; and we shall be so in carrying our own. Agriculture and manufactures have increased with commerce and added to our independence, and will serve to support it if we do not have too much of what is termed the protecting system. Differences will arise in the minds of men how far each should be carried, and legislative power should assist either when it can be done without prejudice to the others; but it is certain that where all are active, and industrious, and intelligent, these things will be kept nearly right, although a few may complain on both sides. It is a subject of great consideration, and should engage the attention of every thinking being, and each should do a part to assist in the great work of building up a nation. We have now some copy of every great and excellent institution that time has produced, though many of them, as yet, are but outlines, and want filling up.

The first step to be taken in order that all the benefits may be derived from the islands of the Pacific which they are capable of affording, must be to spread the light of the gospel and civilization among them, which can only be done through the medium of missionaries. For this purpose I hope I shall not call in vain on my countrywomen, who have contributed so largely in supporting missionary establishments, and other works of charity, both at home and abroad; I implore them to continue their exertions, not only as matters of charity, but of knowledge also, and to assist all in their power to aid the great cause of true national glory. The rising generation are to be educated and directed, and the females of our country have much to do with this. That we possess the requi-

K 3

site capabilities, Hannah More, Miss Edgeworth, Mrs. Hemans,—and our own countrywomen, Mrs. Sigourney and Miss Sedgwick,—may be adduced; and in those branches of which mathematics is the basis, Mrs. Somerville has transcended all who have attempted to instruct youth in these matters before.   A hundred others, on both sides of the water, may be brought forward to prove what women are doing in the great work of advancing the social and intellectual condition of mankind.   This little enterprise of mine—little as it regards society—has taught me what my sex can do if called to act in the business of life.

I feel myself now wedded to the seas as much as the Chief of Venice was to the Adriatic.   I love to contemplate its immensity, its sameness, its power as a medium of communication from one nation to another.   The ocean has all the attributes of sublimity, immensity, and fearfulness; all the properties of usefulness; as affording food for man, and ten thousand pathways for the world. Description cannot reach all its characteristics; the poet who never surveyed the expanse of ocean, and saw only inland waters, has described it the best of all.   Had he seen the Atlantic or the Pacific, in the bosom of their immensity, and felt a little more of that religion which declares that these oceans shall at the judgment give up their dead, he would have added to that description which has never been surpassed in force and beauty :

> " Roll on, thou deep and dark blue ocean, roll !
> Ten thousand fleets sweep over thee in vain ;
> Man marks the earth with ruin—his control
> Stops with the shore.   Upon the watery plain

The wrecks are all thy deed, nor doth remain
A shadow of man's ravage, save his own,
When, for a moment, like a drop of rain,
He sinks into thy depths with bubbling groan,
Without a grave, unknelled, uncoffined, and unknown.

His steps are not upon thy paths; thy fields
Are not a spoil for him.   Thou dost arise
And shake him from thee; the vile strength he wields
For earth's destruction, thou dost all despise,
Spurning him from thy bosom to the skies,
And send'st him, shivering in thy playful spray,
And howling to his gods, where haply lies
His petty hope in some near port or bay,
And dashest him to earth again.   There let him lay.

The armaments which thunder-strike the walls
Of rock-built cities, bidding nations quake
And monarchs tremble in their capitals—
The oak leviathans, whose huge ribs make
Their clay creator the vain title take
Of lord of thee, and arbiter of war:
These are thy toys, and as the snowy flake
They melt into thy yest of waves, which mar
Alike the Armada's pride, or spoils of Trafalgar!

Thy shores are empires, changed in all, save thee,
Assyria, Greece, Rome, Carthage, what are they?
Thy waters wasted them while they were free,
And many a tyrant since; their shores obey
The stranger, slave or savage; their decay
Has dried up realms of deserts: not so thou;
Unchangeable save to thy wild waves' play,
Time writes no wrinkle on thine azure brow;
Such as creation's dawn beheld, thou rollest now.

Thou glorious mirror, where the Almighty's form
Glasses itself in tempests; in all time,
Calm or convulsed, in breeze, or gale, or storm,
Icing the pole, or in the torrid clime
Dark heaving; boundless, endless, and sublime;
The image of eternity; the throne
Of the Invisible; even from out thy slime
The monsters of the deep are made; each zone
Obeys thee; thou goest forth, dread, fathomless, alone;
And I have loved thee, ocean!"

On the 26th day of August we discovered land: it was my own, my native land, and we were making fair progress towards it, but my impatience was such that I could have scolded the Antarctic for being so sluggish, notwithstanding I had, during the whole voyage, loved her as a dear little boat that had carried me safely; and this affection increased as the time passed on. As we approached the harbour of New-York, I could not forbear comparing it with others I had seen. What city in the world is so advantageously placed? Surrounded by rivers, and washed by the sea, its water privileges are everywhere. Europe, nor Asia, nor Africa, nor South America has any thing to compare with it. Its deep waters and its crowded mart of merchandise are unequalled in this country; and when we add to this, the connexion of the great inland seas of the north, it has no rival anywhere. In less than fifty years its population has increased more than tenfold: in 1783 it contained 20,000 inhabitants; it now numbers more than 200,000. Its wealth has increased with its population, and all seemed so busy and happy. A forest of masts appeared on either side of the city, closer together than the cedars of Lebanon in their native soil. The time is fast coming, thought I, when this great city will be ten times greater than it now is, and rival all of ancient or modern times. And this is indeed my home! —my native land.

On the 27th of August I came on shore. As I left the little bark, I could not help exclaiming, Have I been almost two years in that schooner! I had, and was as safe in her, I believe, as I should have been in a seventy-four, if not altogether so comfortable at all times. I now stepped upon the soil of my native city; its spires, its steamboats, its bustle, all delighted me, for it was New-York as I had left it; changed only by increase, and that not so much as to give it in any way a strange look. In a few moments I embraced my child—my mother—my sisters—and some of my friends—and was greeted as one indeed from a far distant country. But on looking around, I saw the emblems of bereavement; my mother was again a widow—her husband, my worthy step-father, had died of a consumption during my absence. He was truly a good man; he had been to me as an own father, he was kind to my mother, and kind to her offspring, which she had brought at her marriage. A dear aunt, too, had in my absence paid the debt of nature. I mingled my tears with those of my surviving relatives, at our loss; but who can expect to find home as it was left, after so long an absence? My mother and my child were alive and well; and I thanked kind Heaven for what had been preserved, while I sincerely mourned the departed. New cares were soon allotted me, for in nine days after my return I was the happy mother of another son, a fine child in form and strength. His mother's Journal may, in some future day, be read by him, and he may be stimulated to put some of my plans in a train of experiment: but all is in the hands of Heaven—the will of the Lord be done.

The public soon caught some fragments of our adventures, and the seaman LEONARD SHAW published his account of the massacre at the newly discovered islands; our story was in every print, and the sympathies of the public were expressed in warm congratulations. Business soon took my husband to the south, and wishing me to accompany him I did so, and was received with kindness

and attention wherever we made any stop. So
many questions were put to me, that I soon after
determined to give my narrative to the public. I
feel grateful to my countrymen and women for the
courtesies I have received from them, but more so
to that Being who, in his infinite mercy, has protected me in every peril, and brought me again to
my native land, to praise him, and to enjoy all the
blessings that land affords. I can sing aloud, with
all my soul, this hymn of praise to him who con-
trols the winds and seas :—

> " Though they through foreign lands should roam,
>   And breathe the tainted air,
> In burning climates, far from home,
>   Yet thou, their God, art there.
>
> Thy goodness sweetens every soil,
>   Makes every country please :
> Thou on the snowy hills dost smile,
>   And smooth'st the rugged seas !
>
> When waves on waves, to heaven upreared,
>   Defied the pilot's art ;
> When terror in each face appeared,
>   And sorrow in each heart ;
>
> To thee I raised my humble prayer,
>   To snatch me from the grave !
> I found thine ear not slow to hear,
>   Nor short thine arm to save !
>
> Thou gavest the word—the winds did cease,
>   The storm obeyed thy will ;
> The raging sea was hushed in peace,
>   And every wave was still !
>
> For this, my life, in every state,
>   A life of praise shall be ;
> And death, when death shall be my fate,
>   Shall join my soul to thee !"

THE END.

For EU product safety concerns, contact us at Calle de José Abascal, 56–1°, 28003 Madrid, Spain or eugpsr@cambridge.org.